THE GOODNESS OF GUINNESS

First published in 2005 by
Liberties Press
Guinness Enterprise Centre | Taylor's Lane | Dublin 8 | Ireland
www.libertiespress.com | info@libertiespress.com
+353 (1) 415 1224

Trade enquiries to CMD Distribution
55A Spruce Avenue | Stillorgan Industrial Park | Blackrock | County Dublin
Tel: +353 (1) 294 2560
Fax: +353 (1) 294 2564

ISBN 978–0–9545335–7–1

2 4 6 8 10 9 7 5 3 1

A CIP record for this title is available from the British Library

Cover design by Dermot Hall
Set in Garamond

Printed by CPD | Ebbw Vale | Wales

THE GOODNESS OF GUINNESS

THE BREWERY, ITS PEOPLE
AND THE CITY OF DUBLIN

TONY CORCORAN

CONTENTS

FOREWORD BY FINBARR FLOOD   7

ABBREVIATED GUINNESS FAMILY TREE   9
ACKNOWLEDGEMENTS   11
INTRODUCTION   15

1   IN THE BEGINNING   21
    The Family History of the Guinnesses   21
    The Guinness Wives   28

2   THE GUINNESS BREWERY IN THE
    NINETEENTH CENTURY   32

3   THE DAWN OF A NEW CENTURY   40
    Conditions in Dublin in 1900   40
    Guinness Families in Dublin in 1900   43
    The Lumsden Inspection of Dwellings   45
    The Follow-up to Lumsden's Inspection   50
    Other Initiatives of Lumsden   52
    Lumsden's Research on Housing   55

4   GUINNESS SOCIAL INITIATIVES
    IN THE TWENTIETH CENTURY   58
    Queen's Day   58
    The Annual Entertainment   60
    The Medical Department   61
    The Battle Against Tuberculosis   66
    The St John Ambulance Brigade   67
    The Great War and 1916   69

5	THE GUINNESS ATHLETIC UNION	72
6	THE IVEAGH TRUST	78
	Thomas Court and the Belview Buildings	80
	The Iveagh Gardens, Crumlin	81
7	THE BREWERY IN THE FORTIES AND FIFTIES	82
	The Blue Book	87
	The Guinness Permanent Building Society	89
	Pay-packet Deductions	90
	The 1959 Bicentenary	90
8	THE PERSONNEL STRUCTURE IN GUINNESS	94
9	INDUSTRIAL RELATIONS IN GUINNESS	105
	The St James's Gate Senior Foremen's Association	107
10	PASSING ON THE CARING	112
	The Social Scene	119
	The Guinness Drama Group	121
	The Guinness Variety Group	125
	The Guinness Choir	125
	The Guinness Film Society	127
	Other Social Activities	128
11	WORKING ON SHIFT	130
	The Belview Dining Rooms	134
	The Taps	134
	Funnels and Tunnels	136
	The Excise Officers	137
	The Appliance of Science	139
	CONCLUSION: LOOKING TO THE FUTURE	143
	ENDNOTES	147
	BIBLIOGRAPHY	153
	INDEX	155

FOREWORD

It gives me great pleasure to be associated with this fascinating book by Tony Corcoran. Tony and I have a number of things in common: we both come from families with strong connections with the Guinness Brewery at St James's Gate and we both had long service working within the company – forty-one years in my case and thirty-eight years in Tony's. I think it is fair to say that such lengthy service will soon be a thing of the past, never mind with one company!

Guinness employees were steeped in the history of the company, the Guinness family and its philanthropic pursuits. Many of us knew personally the last Earl of Iveagh who actually worked in the company: Benjamin, the Third Earl of Iveagh, who died at the all-too-young age of fifty-five in 1992. We also knew at first-hand how the unique policies adopted by the company, such as medical benefits, housing, social clubs, savings and loans clubs and sports facilities benefited not only all the employees and their families but also many other Dublin families and residents.

Tony's research has been a labour of love, which has taken six long years to compile. It is an excellent document not only for general reading purposes but also for students of social history and indeed of Dublin in the 'rare oul' times'.

The Guinness family's generosity and vision is well known among those who worked in the company, but this book will spread that knowledge to many more over the years: it will have appeal for everyone and will serve as a history of a bygone era. As the numbers working in Guinness decline and the longevity of employment decreases, this knowledge will no longer be passed on. It is more essential than ever to commit these important facts to paper, and Tony's book is most timely in that respect.

I heartily congratulate Tony on this fantastic piece of work. It is an outstanding achievement, and I thank him on behalf of all of us who have a profound love for the Guinness family and the company of the past, for taking the time and trouble to put the goodness of Guinness on the record for the future.

Finbarr Flood
Former Managing Director, Guinness Dublin
June 2005

ABBREVIATED GUINNESS FAMILY TREE

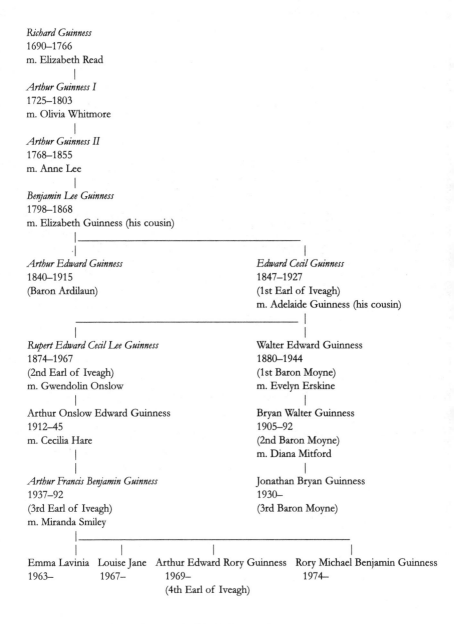

Richard Guinness
1690–1766
m. Elizabeth Read

Arthur Guinness I
1725–1803
m. Olivia Whitmore

Arthur Guinness II
1768–1855
m. Anne Lee

Benjamin Lee Guinness
1798–1868
m. Elizabeth Guinness (his cousin)

Arthur Edward Guinness
1840–1915
(Baron Ardilaun)

Edward Cecil Guinness
1847–1927
(1st Earl of Iveagh)
m. Adelaide Guinness (his cousin)

Rupert Edward Cecil Lee Guinness
1874–1967
(2nd Earl of Iveagh)
m. Gwendolin Onslow

Walter Edward Guinness
1880–1944
(1st Baron Moyne)
m. Evelyn Erskine

Arthur Onslow Edward Guinness
1912–45
m. Cecilia Hare

Bryan Walter Guinness
1905–92
(2nd Baron Moyne)
m. Diana Mitford

Arthur Francis Benjamin Guinness
1937–92
(3rd Earl of Iveagh)
m. Miranda Smiley

Jonathan Bryan Guinness
1930–
(3rd Baron Moyne)

Emma Lavinia
1963–

Louise Jane
1967–

Arthur Edward Rory Guinness
1969–
(4th Earl of Iveagh)

Rory Michael Benjamin Guinness
1974–

(Names given in *italics* are those involved in the brewing line)

DEDICATION

To my mother, Eileen (1909–1992),
who taught me to love books and literature

ACKNOWLEDGEMENTS

With a book like this, which has taken more than six years to prepare, it is difficult to recall the many people who were generous with their comments, information and encouragement, without whose help the study would have been too daunting to complete.

Perhaps, though, on a subliminal level, the study began on the death of my father in 1958, when two people in particular were instrumental in ensuring that the Corcoran links with Guinness continued into another generation. These were Andrew Hughes-Onslow and Stan Corran, who encouraged my application to the company based on my Leaving Cert results. On my first day in the maelstrom of activity that was the Brewers' Lab, one colleague, Tony Moran, took the time to look after me and take me to lunch. Also, within my first week there a friend of my father's, Alex Byrne, took time to give me some fatherly advice. All of these people are now deceased and hopefully sat by my shoulder as I wrote this work.

One colleague who had a unique influence on my whole outlook on life was Des Carrick, whose father, like mine, was a Guinness Supervisor. Des introduced me to the world of art and creativity in all its forms, and it was he who encouraged my fledgling writing ambitions. I was also given the opportunity to write about social life in Guinness by the editors of the two house magazines, Mike Lawlor and Carol Scott. Throughout my career in the brewing departments, I met many people who became not only work colleagues but kindred spirits whose company made life more bearable than it otherwise would have been. Names that come to mind are Charlie McDermott, Peter Walsh, Ted Nulty, Tom (T.A.) Donohoe, Paddy Tucker, Willie Keogh,

Willie Mullen, Anne Lewis and John McMahon. Two of these, Peter Walsh and Willie Mullen, have researched and written much on Guinness history, and I would like to acknowledge how much their work has helped to inspire what I have written.

After retirement, I needed to talk with many people in order to support and build on my memories of Guinness life. I began in 1999 with a visit to Paddy Skelton at his home in Galway. Paddy was a lovely man, now happily tending to vintage cars in the forecourt of heaven. I continued with the previous archivist, Teresa O'Donnell, and moved on to the current archivists, Eibhlin Roche and Clare Hackett. During my research, an engineering colleague, Michael Byrne, shared much of his own research on a parallel topic. Many thanks also to Christy Byrne for material given to me.

At the same time, I spoke with many people, including Paddy Scully, Mick Kiersey, Stan Barnes, Willie O'Connor, John Fitzpatrick, Paddy Murphy and Paddy Connaughton. My ventures into the entertainment world brought me into contact with Ada Kelly of the Guinness Choir and with Yvonne Robins, Audrey Nicholson and Damien Flood of the Guinness Players. As the work progressed, I was helped by Nick and Catherine Pollard, who let me use their house in County Clare for correcting an early draft. Ita O'Gara, Donal Byrne and John Mullins read and corrected drafts for me and, in particular, made constructive amendments to these drafts.

Throughout the writing period, I had many consultations, in person and by e-mail, with Rory Guinness, brother of the present Earl of Iveagh, who was extremely courteous, helpful and encouraging. By far the most important influence for me, however, was Sir John Lumsden, Chief Medical Officer, who joined Guinness in 1894 and died in 1945. It was he who mirrored and enlarged the Guinness-family tradition of *noblesse oblige* and began the practical application of primary care to make employment in the Guinness Brewery a 'womb to tomb' model unequalled anywhere else in the world.

Overall, though, everyone with whom I worked and associated has had an influence on this work. Even though all the names are not written here, I am grateful for their help. Finally, I dedicate this work to my family, past, present and future. I thank the past generation for shaping my life and my present family for their encouragement. To the future generations, I offer this work as a record of past history and values.

Tony Corcoran
May 2005

INTRODUCTION

Whenever I bleed, I am always surprised to see that my blood is not black. Certainly, when you consider that I was born into two Guinness families, had two Guinness grandfathers and five Guinness uncles, and was on the Guinness premises before I could walk, I am as much a product of Guinness as the black stuff itself.

My two grandfathers, Thaddeus Corcoran and John Ennis, both from farming families in south Dublin, one from Bohernabreena, the other from Crumlin, had come to live in the last decade of the nineteenth century in the area now loosely known as the Liberties and had applied for work in the great Guinness Brewery at St James's Gate. Both had presented good references and both had been taken on as labourers in 1891.

Why they both applied to Guinness is easy to understand. At the end of the Victorian era, the city of Dublin was in a depressed state. Living conditions were appalling, and disease was rampant in the high tenement houses, claustrophobic courts and back alleys of the city. Unemployment meant eviction and transfer to the South Dublin Union, the workhouse. In the midst of all this, Guinness had a reputation for being the best employer in the world, offering medical benefits, sick pay and pensions.

Arthur Guinness had come to Dublin from Leixlip in County Kildare in 1759 with a legacy of £100 from his father's employer, Archbishop Price (previously Archbishop of Cashel), a man to whom his father, Richard Guinness, had been steward. He already had some expertise in brewing, having run a small brewery in Leixlip. He purchased the lease on a small, disused brewery at St James's Gate from its previous owner, Mark

Rainsford, and then surveyed the competition. The area boasted more than sixty breweries of various sorts, all of which were reported to have brewed beer of 'indifferent quality'. Arthur was already a convert to the concept of 'quality assurance' and set about brewing ale of high quality, which soon outsold that of all his competitors. He was also a good judge of character and quickly built up a sizeable workforce of loyal and motivated labourers.

Over the following two hundred years, the Guinness family became employers of people who shared their commitment to quality. They were deeply religious and ethical and, at the same time, astute businessmen. They believed, as did many employers of the time, in the principle of *noblesse oblige*: in sharing their wealth with those who had helped them achieve it. They were generous not only to their workers but also to the city of Dublin.

In 1886, five years before Thaddeus Corcoran and John Ennis joined Guinness, the company had been put on the stock exchange and had been incorporated. While ownership was now in the hands of the shareholders, the management and direction of the company were still firmly in the hands of the Guinness family. From 1890 onwards, however, the social history of the company and its workers, at all levels, took on a significance that was to mirror the emergence of the Irish state several decades later.

In 1890, the Guinness Trust, later to become the Iveagh Trust, was set up. This organisation was set up in 1890 by Edward Cecil Guinness, using his own fortune, for the construction of working-class housing at affordable rents. Eighteen ninety-four marked the entry into the company's medical department of a junior doctor who was to have a special influence on the lives of those who worked for the company. Dr John Lumsden became Chief Medical Officer in 1898 and, by 1900, had instigated a series of inspections of homes to ensure that all Guinness workers lived in proper housing. He later began a study of diets to ensure adequate nourishment for all; this initiative led to the establishment of classes in cookery for the Guinness wives. Working on the basis that the women in the home had an influence not only on the diets of their families but on the family culture, he introduced a series of concerts exclusively for women, to raise their cultural standards.

Within the workforce, he was working aggressively to overcome the dreaded tuberculosis in young people; he was a major mover in founding and financing the Royal Hospital for Consumptives in Newcastle, County Wicklow. He toured Germany and Switzerland to learn about the health spas that were used in Europe to counter tuberculosis. He also visited the housing estates that English industrialists such as Cadburys, Rowntrees and Levers had built for their workers.

It was mainly through the efforts of John Lumsden that the first Guinness sports club – the St James's Gate Athletic and Cycling Union – was set up in 1905. This was to be the focal point for a range of sports clubs which followed later. A football club followed, then a gymnasium, and then a boxing club and a tug-of-war team. Over the next twenty-five years, the Guinness Athletic Union came into being with the donation by Lord Iveagh of a dedicated Guinness sports ground in Crumlin. Bowling, cricket, lawn tennis and table tennis became popular pastimes for the Guinness workers and their families.

The Iveagh Grounds in Crumlin was to become the centre for social activity amongst Guinness workers and their families. There was keen participation, as well as interdepartmental rivalry, in the various sports, and, most importantly, there was social activity amongst the workers' families who visited the grounds as spectators and enjoyed the fresh air of what was then the countryside of Crumlin. Indeed, at one stage there was opposition to the siting of the grounds at Crumlin because, as a consultant employed to investigate the feasibility of the project put it, 'the trams didn't go there'.

Thus it was that the Corcorans and the Ennises, along with the Byrnes, the Hugheses, the O'Tooles, and hundreds of other Guinness families, began to socialise. There was a unique sense of belonging, of being part of the extended Guinness family.

Romances began and marriages took place. There was little need to investigate the background of either partner: they were all well known to each other, and the medical department had the medical records of every one of them!

It was against this cultural background that my parents met, and were married in 1938, and into which I was born in 1940. We lived in a quiet avenue off Donore Avenue, then a narrow cobbled street dominated by a stud farm and exercise stables for a collection of prize show horses. Beyond that was the forbidding wall of Cork Street Fever Hospital, which served to quicken the pace to Cork Street and Marrowbone Lane, where the wisps of blue smoke from Plunkett's Roasthouse stung your eyes before you entered Robert Street, Belview and the Guinness 'Back Gate'.

Before I could walk, I remember being wheeled to the junction of Belview to meet my father coming out through the Back Gate. Even as a toddler, I sensed that the two huge pillars of the gate had some significance. Occasionally, as a special treat, I was wheeled through the narrow entrance beside the gate into the Time Office, where the men handed in their brass numbers at the window and collected them on the way out. It was a world of huge men who leaned down to speak to me with breath that smelt of beer and yeast. In later years, as a toddler, I was taken by the hand into the Workmen's Recreation Rooms in Belview to meet my father in the Reading Rooms, where the magazine table was made available for me to look at the pictures in the *Illustrated London News* of the bombed streets of London in World War II. In particular, photographs of distressed and starving people all over Europe influenced my emerging sense of justice. I became aware, even at such a young age, of the evils of war and resolved never to waste food – an awareness I continue to carry to this day.

Another special treat was, of course, to be brought to the Iveagh Grounds. It was off the main road, so I was allowed to roam around the grounds. I wandered in and out of the pavilion, through the shower rooms, which smelt of carbolic soap, and the dressing rooms, which smelt of sweat. I went out onto the tennis courts and wound the nets up and down, to flush out the earwigs that lived in the ratchet equipment. Then, when I began to feel bored, I wandered into the bar. There I met my uncles (and a few adopted uncles as well) and talked to them until the head barman spotted me and I was moved to outside the door. This always had its rewards, as I was never put out without being given a huge pint glass of orange squash, which I drank slowly, using both hands, and enjoying the pinch on my nose as the gas from the squash caught my breath.

Even at home, the atmosphere was one of 'the Brewery'. We lived next door to my uncle's family, where even the gossip over the back wall was about other Brewery families. Once, I was the unwitting carrier of a practical joke. My father had engaged a Brewery carpenter to fix our back gate as a 'nixer'. As the carpenter worked away, I was playing on the road when I was called in by a neighbour, also a Guinness worker. 'Ask Mr Murphy' (not his real name), I was instructed, 'if there's any news.' Dutifully, I carried out the task. It wasn't until many years later that I learnt that Mr Murphy had been married a few months previously!

I didn't realise until I went to school that a world existed outside of Guinness. It was then that I began to mix in a wider circle, with boys whose fathers didn't work for Guinness – indeed, who didn't work at all. It was just after World War II, and many of the boys had fathers working in England. As for me, I was, unwittingly, the envy of many, with my long pencils with 'Guinness' stamped on them in gold, which I had pinched from my father's pocket. I was also too young to realise that, whenever anyone in the family was ill, the Guinness doctor would be called and we didn't have to pay.

Bit by bit, as I grew older I began to realise the importance of being part of both a Guinness family and the ordered world of 'the Brewery'. My family and I were part of a huge social order which had a significant impact on the social life of Dublin. At any one time, there were thousands of people of all ages in receipt of 'the goodness of Guinness'.

As Ireland is now a more capitalist and, some would say, less caring, consumerist society, it is time to look back in tribute at the caring society that is the legacy of Victorian Dublin and, especially, the Guinness family.

1

IN THE BEGINNING

THE FAMILY HISTORY OF THE GUINNESSES

After almost three centuries, it must be acknowledged that there exists in the Guinness family a unique set of qualities. These include an astute business sense, appreciation of the efforts of others, enquiring minds, patronage of the arts, theatre and literature, a scientific approach to agriculture, broadly humanitarian qualities and, above all, benevolence and a respect for religion.

It has been said that the Guinnesses regarded their wealth as a gift from God and, as such, it was to be used for the benefit of mankind and not squandered. There are reports of the second Arthur Guinness beginning and ending the day with family prayers, and an entire branch of the Guinness family ran missions in the East End of London and travelled as missionaries to the Congo and China.

So, where did it all begin? The name 'Guinness' first appeared with Richard Guinness, father of the first Arthur Guinness. Efforts to trace the family back beyond that have been unsuccessful. There are two schools of thought on the more distant origins of the name. Firstly, there was an officer of Cromwell's army called 'Ghennis', originally from Cornwall. Over the years, the Ghennis family have made contact with the Guinness family and, although they were received with courtesy, no formal links with them were ever made, or continued.

Secondly, there is a more formal link with the Magennis clan of County Down, believed to be related to the O'Neills. This is the link favoured by the Guinness family. The Magennises fought at the Battle of the Boyne on the side of King James – the Catholic side. The Magennis base was in a place called Iveagh in County Down. Many years later, Edward Cecil Guinness took the title 'Earl of Iveagh'; the Guinness coat of arms is a derivation of the Magennis coat of arms.

So how can there be a link between the Catholic Magennis clan in County Down in 1690 and the Guinness family, servants to the Protestant Archbishop of Cashel, a hundred years later? We begin with Richard Guinness, father of the first Arthur Guinness. Richard's birth details are unknown, and our first knowledge of this humble man is as steward to Archbishop Arthur Price in Celbridge, County Kildare. The duties of a steward at that time included looking after household provisions – and brewing small amounts of household beer. So, the first brewing Guinness was Richard, who brewed beer as part of his household duties. No doubt he passed his brewing skills on to his first-born and eldest son, Arthur. Richard and his wife, Elizabeth Read, had six children in total: Arthur, Frances, Elizabeth, Benjamin, Richard and Samuel. The youngest son, Samuel, became a goldsmith and the ancestor of the banking side of the Guinness family.[1]

It is said that the Archbishop of Cashel became renowned as a host, not least for the quality of the dark beer he served to his guests. When he died in 1752, he left £100 to his servant Richard, who used the money to set up a local hostelry in Celbridge called the 'Bear and Ragged Staff'. Young Arthur was then twenty-seven years old, and the Archbishop also left him £100. Using this legacy, Arthur set up his first brewery – not in Dublin, but in Leixlip, County Kildare. Then, having brewed a beer remarkable for its quality for three years, he left the Leixlip brewery in the hands of his younger brother, Richard, and set out for Dublin.

When Arthur Guinness took on the ailing brewery at St James's Gate from Mark Rainsford in 1759, he already had a great deal of expertise, both in business and in brewing, and was a mature thirty-four years of age. With the brewery came a nice town house, No. 1 Thomas Street, into which the new Mr Guinness settled. He quickly became a businessman and a social mover of some note. Within two years, he had met and proposed marriage to Olivia Whitmore, ward of William Lunell and a cousin of the great orator and parliamentarian Henry Grattan. On 17 June 1761, the couple were married; Olivia brought an inheritance of £1,000 – a huge sum at the time- to the marriage. Equally important, she was very well-connected in Dublin society.

Obviously believing in the wisdom of large families, Olivia became pregnant twenty-one times over the course of twenty-six years, resulting in a family of six sons and four daughters. Their first-born, Elizabeth, later married Frederick Darley, who became Lord Mayor of Dublin in 1809. The second child was a son, Hosea, born in 1765. He took Holy Orders, married a woman named Jane Hart and was the first of a long line of Guinnesses to enter the church. He was for thirty years rector of St Werburgh's Church, located next to Dublin Castle, and Chancellor of St Patrick's Cathedral. Hosea's youngest son, Francis Hart Vicesimus Guinness, emigrated first to India and then to New Zealand, where many of his descendants live to this day.[2]

Their third child, born in 1768, was a son, Arthur, later known as Arthur Guinness of Beaumont. He lived in the family home at Beaumont, several miles north of Dublin. In 1794, he married Anne Lee, and they had three sons. Meanwhile, his father (the first Arthur) died at his town house in Gardiner Street aged seventy-eight. His funeral took place on 23 January 1803. The funeral cortège travelled from Beaumont, an elegant white Georgian manor house, to the graveyard at Oughterard in County Kildare, where he was laid beside his mother, Elizabeth Read.

The second Arthur took over the business on his father's death; he was assisted by his brother Benjamin and by William

Lunell. Arthur was also a director of the Bank of Ireland and in 1820 became its Governor. As early as 1797, he is reported as publicly supporting Daniel O'Connell and the cause of Catholic Emancipation.

Of the three sons of the second Arthur, the eldest, William Smythe Lee Grattan Guinness, went into the church, and the second, Artur Lee, had little interest in the business. The third son, Benjamin Lee Guinness, however, had entered the brewery at age sixteen in 1814 and worked there for forty years, until the death of his father in 1855. The second Arthur is laid to rest in the family vault at Mount Jerome Cemetery in Dublin with the simple inscription: 'Arthur Guinness of Beaumont, County Dublin'.[3]

Prior to taking over the business in 1855, Benjamin Lee Guinness had been active in business and social circles. He lived at St Anne's in Clontarf, on the east side of Dublin, and had been elected Lord Mayor of Dublin in 1851. In 1856, he purchased No. 80 St Stephen's Green as his town house, in the centre of Dublin, overlooking the fashionable private park. In 1865, he was elected Conservative MP for Dublin city, a post he held until his death in 1868. Also in 1865, at a cost of £150,000 of his own money, he renovated St Patrick's Cathedral in Dublin, which was in danger of becoming a ruin. For this and 'other public service', he was created a baronet in 1867. He began a huge programme of investment in the brewery at St James's Gate.[4] As a family, the Guinnesses' surroundings were described as opulent, but their lives were sober and their days began and ended with family prayers.

Sir Benjamin Lee Guinness died in London at the age of seventy on 19 May 1868 and the family business was bequeathed to his two sons, Sir Arthur Edward, who inherited his father's baronetcy and parliamentary seat, and Edward Cecil. Included in the terms of Sir Benjamin Lee's will was the stipulation that the family fortune should remain concentrated in the brewery.[5] After some years, Arthur Edward, later to become Lord Ardilaun, sold his interest in the business to his brother, Edward Cecil. This left

Arthur Edward free to pursue his real interests: public life and philanthropy. He is reported to have given the impression that he gave money away not to please others but to please himself. He completed the reconstruction of Marsh's Library beside St Patrick's Cathedral – work which his father had begun – and rebuilt the Coombe Lying-in Hospital. He later became chairman of the Dublin Artisans' Dwelling Company, the first Dublin organisation to concern itself with the housing of workers. He purchased from the residents the lovely twenty-two-acre park at St Stephen's Green, which was overlooked by his brother's town house, and paid to have the park redesigned and a pond installed – and presented it to the citizens of Dublin.[6]

As an aside, members of the Guinness family had a diverse range of business interests. A grandson of Sir Benjamin Lee, through his second son Lee, was Kenelm Lee Guinness, a successful racing motorist who invented a special form of spark plug which he named using his own initials, K.L.G., and which was later manufactured on a commercial scale.[7]

Edward Cecil Guinness, later to be created baronet (1885), baron (1891), viscount (1904) and the first Lord Iveagh (1919), was a remarkable man who had a great concern for people.[8] After 1874, when he had assumed sole proprietorship of the company, he made many changes in the terms of employment of his workers. Amongst these was, in 1881, the purchase of Kingsbridge Woollen Mills for the purpose of creating employment for the daughters of Guinness workers, thereby indirectly benefiting the family income. Sadly, after about eight years in operation, the mills were closed down due to serious economic difficulties. Around the same time, he modernised the structure of the company, and he launched it on the stock market in 1886.

One of his acquisitions, after taking over the brewery in 1874, was the purchase of Farmleigh, a substantial property overlooking the Phoenix Park. This enabled him and his wife to entertain on a grand scale, in addition to entertaining at his town house at 80 St Stephen's Green. Living at Farmleigh allowed him to stroll through the park to visit either the Woollen Mills at

Kingsbridge or the Brewery at St James's Gate.

One of the concerns of Edward Cecil was affordable housing, not just for Guinness workers but for all the ordinary workers of the time – the artisans who were the skilled manual workers of Dublin. He divided his time between London and Dublin and was instrumental in setting up the Dublin Artisans' Dwelling Company, along with the Earl of Meath. In Rialto, beside the Brewery, he contracted the Dublin Artisans' Dwelling Company to build a housing scheme in 1883 for renting at affordable prices to Guinness workers.

By far the greatest achievement of Edward Cecil, however, was the establishment in 1890 of the Guinness Trust, a major philanthropic trust to provide affordable housing for the labouring classes – not just Guinness workers – of Dublin and London. The Trust was founded with an endowment of £250,000 (around €20 million in today's money): £200,000 of this sum was to provide housing in London, and £50,000 in Dublin. In later years, he was to invest further sums in the Dublin operation.[9]

In 1903, the two funds were separated. The Dublin operation became known as the Iveagh Trust, which went on to construct various buildings that are well known to Dublin people, including the Iveagh Hostel, the Iveagh Baths, the Bull Alley Play Centre (known as 'the Beano') and housing projects in Crumlin and Rathmines. Another important project was the clearance of a slum area beside St Patrick's Cathedral and its transformation into a public park. Then, as the clearance had disrupted many small merchants and shopkeepers, he had constructed at the north end of Francis Street the Iveagh Market, where clothes and goods could be displayed and sold in airy, clean locations.

Back in London, Edward Cecil endowed the Lister Institute of Preventive Medicine and, with Sir Ernest Cassel, founded the Radium Institute. In 1921, he established the Chadacre Agricultural Institute near Bury St Edmunds to provide training in agriculture for the sons of farm labourers.[10] In 1925, he bought Kenwood, a large house on Hampstead Heath, as a gallery to house his ever-increasing art collection. The gallery, now known as the Iveagh Bequest, along with the house and surrounding land, passed by the terms of his will to the London County Council.[11]

In 1873, just before he took over the family business, Edward Cecil had married his second cousin, Adelaide Guinness, known as 'Dodo'. Adelaide was a great-granddaughter of Samuel Guinness, brother of the first Arthur Guinness, and was, therefore, from the Guinness banking line. Their first child, born in 1874, was a son, Rupert Edward Cecil Lee Guinness, later to become the second Lord Iveagh and chairman of the company until his death in 1967. Their second son was Walter Edward, later to be Lord Moyne, who was assassinated in Cairo while acting as British Consul in 1944. Walter Edward's son, Bryan Guinness, the Second Lord Moyne, later became a popular and colourful vice-chairman of the Guinness board of directors.

While Edward Cecil is remembered in a plaque in the front yard of the Brewery, his son Rupert is commemorated in the theatre built at St James's Gate in 1951: the Rupert Guinness Hall. Rupert was a quiet, shy person, who, nonetheless, excelled at Cambridge University, both academically and at rowing, winning the Diamond Sculls in 1895. He was an MP from 1908 until his father's death in 1927, when he inherited the title Earl of Iveagh and the chairmanship of the company.

Rupert spent a great deal of time at the family home at Elveden in Surrey and was an enthusiastic farmer who instigated many research projects. He and his wife, Gwendolin Onslow, were regular and hospitable hosts to King Edward, who took part in many enjoyable shooting parties at Elveden. They had five children, Richard, Lady Honor, Arthur Onslow Edward, Lady Patricia and Lady Brigid. Arthur Onslow Edward, born in 1912, became Viscount Elveden. After his death in 1945, the title went to his eldest son, Arthur Francis Benjamin, who was born in 1937.

Thus it was that, in 1967, when Rupert Guinness died, the

title Third Earl of Iveagh passed to his grandson, Arthur Francis Benjamin, more commonly known as Benjamin. Benjamin was one of the less fortunate Guinnesses in that, not only did he have to cope with serious illness for most of his life, but he had to deal with the rationalisation of the company during the 1980s. In order to do this, he sought the assistance of Ernest Saunders, a world-renowned marketing executive from the Nestlé Corporation, in 1981.

Benjamin Guinness, Third Earl of Iveagh, married Miranda Smiley in 1962 and they had four children – Emma Lavinia, Louisa Jane, Arthur Edward Rory and Rory Michael Benjamin. In 1992, thirty years after their wedding, Benjamin Guinness died and the title Fourth Earl of Iveagh passed to their eldest son, Arthur Edward – known as Ned Guinness.

The same year, 1992, saw the death also of Bryan Guinness, Lord Moyne and former vice-chairman of the Brewery. Following these deaths there was no longer a Guinness name on the board of the Guinness company.

Although it has virtually disappeared from the boardrooms in Dublin and London, the Guinness name is obviously still in use as a brand name for beer produced at Dublin, London and overseas. Most importantly, the Guinness family maintains a deep and active presence in the multitude of benevolent organisations to which they subscribed over the past two hundred and forty-five years – the Iveagh Trust, the Guinness Trust, the Lister Institute and many others.

THE GUINNESS WIVES

Over a period of almost two hundred and fifty years, the name of Guinness has come to be associated with Irishness, quality, generosity and business acumen, qualities summed up in the company's marketing slogan of the early twentieth century: 'Guinness is Good for You'. Behind this formidable dynasty lay nine generations of Guinness men with many characteristics in common. They were astute, God-fearing men, generous, with a huge sense of responsibility to their communities. They were clever, some were manipulative, all were studious, energetic, questioning, and superb managers of their business. Yet, throughout the generations there were complex personalities and a continuous streak of shyness.

From what we read, therefore, the Guinness wives were exceptional women of strong character. Olivia Whitmore, the wife of the first Arthur Guinness, was a cousin of the great parliamentarian Henry Grattan. She was also the ward of William Lunnel. Firstly, she must have had great physical strength to have survived twenty-one pregnancies. Most importantly, she contributed to the strong spiritual and religious theme through her eldest son, Hosea, thus beginning the foundations of the Grattan Guinnesses, a dynasty of religious leaders, preachers, missionaries and friends of the underpriveleged people of London, New Zealand, Africa and China. There is no doubt that the great skills in oratory of Henry Grattan lived on in the 'Church Guinnesses' many of whom were in great demand as preachers. Indeed, there are still Guinnesses involved in the church in Britain, New Zealand and Australia.

The next Guinness wife of note was Anne Lee, wife of the second Arthur, who married her in 1793. This was a period in the Guinness business when cashflow presented serious difficulties. When Arthur's eldest brother, Hosea, had entered the church, he was experiencing financial difficulties. Thus, at all levels, the family was going through a difficult time financially. Many nephews of Arthur expected apprenticeships in the Brewery, though not all were suitable. Thus, Anne Lee had to support her husband, who was a renowned charitable man, through all these difficulties. After Hosea had bought a large house at Beaumont in north County Dublin, he found he could not afford to run it, and sold it to Arthur; Anne Lee then became the mistress of Beaumont. After almost twenty-five years of marriage, having borne three sons and six daughters, Anne Lee died.[12]

Unsurprisingly, therefore – and much to the concern of Arthur, who was acutely aware of the lack of financial rewards associated with following a religious calling – many members of the family entered the church. The next generation involved in managing the family business was established when Arthur's youngest son, Benjamin Lee, married his first cousin, Bessie, daughter of the bankrupt Edward Guinness, recently deceased. Arthur favoured his new daughter-in-law, who was a devout Christian and a worshipper at Bethesda Chapel in Dorset Street, a Methodist place of worship opened in the eighteenth century. From that union was born the next generation which included Anne, who married William Conyngham, later the Fourth Baron Plunkett and Archbishop of Dublin. The youngest of that family was Edward Cecil, who married his second cousin, Adelaide, daughter of Richard Guinness of the banking wing of the family.

Adelaide Guinness, at the time of her marriage, had been groomed by her mother Katherine to marry into the aristocracy. She had been presented at the court of her uncle, the Duc de Montebello, and had been well tutored in the art and skills of entertaining. Katherine was displeased that Adelaide chose to marry her common cousin, a brewer, and not a member of the aristocracy. Edward Cecil had by then become a regular patron of the London season of aristocratic parties and outings and was keen to launch himself into the highest levels of society. They were perfectly matched. Adelaide was described as 'petite, vivacious and neat' and was reputed to be a charming hostess. Very soon, they earned a reputation for superb entertaining at their Dublin homes, 80 St Stephen's Green and Farmleigh.[13] Tales abounded of the entertainments at Farmleigh, which inevitably preceded the London season, and they opened Farmleigh to their friends at the time of the racing at Punchestown. There are many stories told of the ballroom decorations at the St Stephen's Green house: it is said that the hundreds of candles in the chandeliers produced so much heat that ladies fainted! We are also told that the table decorations included many ice sculptures, no doubt to counteract the great heat! A commentator of the time refers to the great shame in Dublin social circles not to be invited to Mrs Guinness's ball.[14]

Edward Cecil and Adelaide had three children, Rupert, Walter Edward and Arthur Ernest. Their first son, Rupert Edward Cecil Lee, later the Second Earl of Iveagh, was born at 5 Berkeley Square in London in 1874, a year after their marriage. Arthur Ernest was born in 1876, and Walter Edward, later the First Lord Moyne, in 1880.

Rupert, who inherited his father's title and became Chairman of the company, married Gwendolin Onslow, eldest daughter of the Fourth Earl of Onslow, in 1903. In the same year, Walter Edward married Lady Evelyn Erskine, third daughter of the Fourteenth Earl of Buchan. Later, Arthur Ernest married Marie Clotilde Russell, daughter of Sir George Russell. Arthur Ernest and Clotilde, known as Cloe, set up home at Knockmaroon beside the Phoenix Park in Dublin, close to Farmleigh and close, also, to the Brewery, where Arthur Ernest, known as Ernest, was Managing Director.[15]

2

THE GUINNESS BREWERY

IN THE NINETEENTH CENTURY

Not much is known about employment in the Guinness Brewery at St James's Gate for the first eighty years of its existence. The business was, essentially, a family business run by the family for the family. At the same time, expert brewers were employed to assist the family in producing what was obviously a quality product.

The original Arthur brought his own expertise to St James's Gate from his other brewery in Leixlip. It is likely that some of his Leixlip workers were employed at his new business. As the original plant covered only four acres and included the house, No. 1 Thomas Street, he would have required housekeeping staff, coopers, cleaners and stable workers. The success of the operation points to a meticulously run operation and well-managed partnerships with carefully selected employees.

Certainly one successful partnership was with the Pursers. John Purser originally came from Tewkesbury to brew beer for a James Farrell in Dublin in 1776. His son, also John Purser, came to work for Guinness in 1799 as chief clerk and quickly acquired a position of importance in the company. In turn, his son became an apprentice brewer and by 1820 appears to have been a senior partner in the company, along with the Guinness brothers and William Lunell Guinness. When John Purser died in 1858, his position – but not his partnership – was taken over by his son, John Tertius Purser, then Head Brewer.[16]

Between then and the death of Sir Benjamin Lee Guinness in 1868, a staffing structure emerged, with brewing control in the hands of the Guinnesses and the Pursers, while the actual supervision and administration was conducted by clerks. Around this time, the title 'Senior Night Clerk' came to be used. One interesting name within the rank of the clerks was Dionysius Lardner Boursiquot, reported to be a friend of some of the Guinnesses. After some time, he left Guinness to become an actor in London, initially under the name Lee Morton; later, under yet another name, Dion Boucicault, he wrote a number about plays of Irish life, the most famous of which was *The Colleen Bawn*.[17]

In the 1860s, the two distinct groups of brewers and clerks were recruited mainly from Guinness and Purser connections. In 1870, the leading brewers were Edward Cecil's cousins George and Edmond Waller and John Tertius Purser's two nephews, Thomas Grace Geoghegan and William Purser Geoghegan. The latter became Head Brewer on George Waller's retirement in 1880. Another two nephews, Edward Purser and Samuel Geoghegan, became Head Brewers in their turn.

Thus, by 1890, important positions were held by the Geoghegans and Pursers, all of whom were connected with or related to the Guinnesses. The Head Brewer – who did all the hiring and firing – was William Purser Geoghegan, while Samuel Geoghegan, as Chief Engineer, oversaw a huge expansion of the brewery premises.

A substantial area of land between James's Street and the River Liffey was bought in 1873, and a maltings, a new cooperage and a racking facility were erected there. This facilitated the movement of casks from the racking plant to barges on the river and the transportation of the casks down-river to the port, where they were loaded into ships to be exported to serve the ever-increasing market for Guinness beer overseas.[18]

Samuel was responsible for much of the steelwork of No. 2 Brewery, erected by Spences of Cork Street. His major contribution to the business was the narrow-gauge railway system. He designed the tracks, the steam engines, the bogies and, in a great feat of engineering, the spiral tunnel from the Upper Level to the Lower Level of the brewery. This was a rail tunnel which connected the main yard with the area north of James's Street. As the main yard was fifty feet above the main area north of James's Street, it was necessary to design the tunnel in a spiral, which gradually altered the level without causing the train to accelerate forwards by its own mass.

Little is recorded about the manual workers in the Guinness brewery in the nineteenth century. We know that they joined the company after basic schooling and worked until illness or death overtook them. Certainly, the Guinness family had no need to advertise for workers. They followed a well-established procedure: if the employment at senior level could be conducted so successfully using family connections, the same would apply to the connections of families of loyal and hard-working labourers. In those times, loyalty was as important as hard work. Indeed, in the days of Benjamin Lee, there is recorded, in 1866, an address from the workers to Benjamin Lee, signed by more than five hundred employees, four brewers and forty-nine office gentlemen, making clear their abhorrence of the growing tide of Fenianism:

> We desire especially at this time to express our abhorrence of those sentiments of sedition and rebellion. . . . We believe it to be the duty of true Irishmen to use all their influence to put down and expel from amongst us such mad and pernicious doctrines.

Benjamin Lee replied with thanks and praised their sentiments and their

> fixed resolve to resist the machinations of those wicked and worthless adventurers who would not only deprive our country of the advantages which, as part of the British Empire, we enjoy, but who would overturn all the social arrangements of society . . . would deluge our country in bloodshed and reduce the industrial classes to want and misery.[19]

Indeed, the industrial classes, particularly the Guinness workers, were heartened by the words and support of one of Ireland's greatest industrialists.

In working-class Dublin in the latter part of the nineteenth century, to be employed by Mr Guinness was indeed a privilege. Particularly in the aftermath of the Great Famine, Dublin was an overcrowded city with serious problems relating to poverty and disease.[20] A permanent job was a godsend; a permanent job which paid sick pay and widows' pensions was beyond the imagination of most. Guinness appointed a medical officer in 1869 and opened a dispensary in Bellevue Buildings. Within ten years, a 'Lady Visitor' – who would today be known as a social worker or community nurse – was appointed to look after widows and orphans, and to act as paymistress for pensions. She may also have been responsible for employees who were sick and received half-pay. (This increased to three-quarters pay if the employee was married, and there was discretion to pay the three-quarter rate to unmarried men who were supporting other family members.)

In 1890, the Head Brewer, William Geoghegan, received applications from my two grandfathers, amongst many others. The handwritten references they presented may have had an influence on the fact that they were successful in their applications. Both references are in copperplate handwriting: one from a doctor at Kimmage Lodge and the other from a local merchant in Thomas Street. The format of each is similar: the referee states that he has a personal knowledge of the applicant and testifies to his character. This appears to have been the successful formula for getting a job in the Guinness brewery at the time. At the level of tradesmen and coopers, there seems to have been a 'closed shop', with only the sons of incumbents being employed.

After 1890, there was an effort by the manager with responsibility for labour relations, Renny Tailyour, to specify physical attributes for those being employed. As the bulk of the work in the brewery was physical labour, this was obviously a positive development. Drawing on the experience of the British Army, the relationship between height, weight and chest measurements were specified. Ability to read and write was also checked, but lack of ability in this respect does not appear to have been a drawback. There was also a medical check, mainly concerned with physique, teeth, hearing and sight. Despite the increasing focus on particular attributes, a sympathetic approach was taken to the sons of employees, whose records were marked as such. In 1898, a company rule that a new employee should be 5 feet 9 inches in height and a minimum weight of 11 stone 2 pounds was implemented. In the case of sons of employees, however, the minimum weight was reduced to 9 stone 12 pounds.[21]

Employment procedures were not formalised until 1874, when the Registry Department started to keep a formal book of employees. The rules governing employment was eventually stated in a formal instruction issued in 1903, which stated that a prospective employee 'must be of good physique, well recommended, pass the employment board and supply evidence of age'.

The wages paid to employees remained fairly constant during the mid-1800s, with twelve shillings a week being paid in 1849, thirteen shillings in 1854, and fourteen shillings in 1871, with further gradual increases to eighteen shillings a week in 1882. By 1890, an employee could expect to earn up to twenty-five shillings a week on a normal grade or list. The night allowance, formalised in 1907, was five shillings a month, and overtime was paid at fivepence an hour. There was also a burial allowance of £3 for an employee and £2 for an employee's widow. The lists began in 1889, with a worker starting on the B list and, after a trial period of one year (during which one shilling a week was withheld), being transferred to the A list.[22] Special posts outside the grading structure included those of Caretaker of Workmens' Dwellings, Attendant in Visitors Rooms (female), Attendant at Baths, Bellvue (female) and Housekeeper and Maid at the Medical Department.

By 1891, an employee was defined as 'a person receiving a

weekly wage', and various allowances, such as clothing allowances, were formalised. An Annual Excursion had been introduced in 1886 at the time of incorporation; this was later defined as one day off a year 'for the purpose of enabling [employees] to enjoy a day in the country'. For these days away, the employee was given a rail ticket and spending money for themselves and their families. Single men were allowed take a 'companion'. Stern warnings accompanied these indulgences, however. The employee was expected 'to behave in all cases in an orderly manner, and will be especially careful not to injure the property of any gentleman who may kindly throw open their demesnes for their recreation.'[23]

A General Purposes Subcommittee was set up in 1886 at director level, to deal with the general day-to-day management of the company. The first meeting of the subcommittee was held on Saturday 20 November 1886 and was attended by Sir E. C. Guinness, R. B. Guinness, James R. Stewart Junior and Claude Guinness. Among the many items approved at meetings from this time were pension payments, mainly to widows. There are references to gratuities, coal, bread, and tickets with which flannel for clothing could be purchased at a reduced rate. In some cases, the subcommittee dealt with requests from widows to commute pensions. A typical request was one from a lady who requested that her pension of five shillings a week be commuted to a lump sum of £47 to enable her to emigrate. Another example involved a Gate Porter seeking a sum of £50 to enable him to emigrate to New South Wales.[24]

Other meetings of the committee dealt with various misdemeanours of workers and staff. Words like 'defalcation' abound to describe behaviour which, in those days, led to instant dismissal. In one case, at a very senior level one gentleman was encouraged, in 1891, 'to take a sea voyage' and, in the meantime, to pay personally for his replacement.[25] In 1896, the Truck Act, with set fines for drunkenness, absence, lateness, neglect of duties, smoking, idleness and insubordination, came into being.[26]

There is a reference to waste ground at Rialto Buildings being let to a man for grazing purposes at a rent of £5 per annum, with agreement to terminate at a week's notice. Later, in 1888, there is reference to the letting of garden plots at Rialto. In 1889, the whole site at Rialto was sold to the Dublin Artisans' Dwelling Company.

Critical decisions taken in the closing decade of the nineteenth century include the employment of boys, agreed on 27 October 1887, and the holding of competitive examinations for No. 1 Clerks, on 21 January 1890. Other important decisions covered the formal granting of donations for charitable purposes – which had in the past presumably come directly from the Guinness family. In April 1897, it was decided to donate £3000 to Queen Victoria's Diamond Jubilee Fund: '£2300 to Irish causes and £700 to English causes'.

On 26 June 1888, a decision was made to reorganise the Medical Department and to appoint a full-time midwife for the wives of Guinness workers. The midwife was allowed to reside free of charge in Bellevue Buildings. Around the same time, a contract sanitary inspector was appointed to inspect the houses of employees for a fee of five shillings per house. This inspection was taken over, twelve years later, by the Chief Medical Officer, Dr John Lumsden, and was to become the focus of an intense social study by him.

Decisions were also taken regarding the capital purchase and installation of new plant. There is reference at the meeting of 21 May 1896 to the purchase of four tanks for vathouse drawings (residues) from Ross and Walpole for an estimated £413 and of a laboratory at No. 2 Brewery in 1897 at an estimated cost of the substantial sum of £666. Later, there is approval for a spiral staircase to the laboratory, also to be made by Ross and Walpole, for £32. In 1899, an estimate for £6100 was approved for the erection of workmen's dwellings at Thomas Court. The most significant capital item of the generation, however, was to come in 1903: the new Fermentation Storehouse in Robert Street, the structure of which was designed by Sir William Arrol.[27] This

Storehouse housed the Fermentation Department until the late 1980s; in the 1990s it was converted into the Guinness Visitors' Centre.

A number of significant appointments were made in the closing decade of the nineteenth century. Dr John Lumsden was appointed a junior doctor on 5 March 1894. Two apprentice brewers, Alan McMullan and T. B. Case, were appointed in September 1895. In 1898, T. D. Lambert was appointed the company veterinarian surgeon, and in 1899 Henry Deanesly was made an assistant in the Engineers Department. At the same time, Mr C. E. Dockery – who was later to be shot dead in a tragic accident on Brewery premises in 1916 – was appointed a night clerk. Other appointments at the time were Mr Forbes Watson, a chemist who devised a means of extracting barm beer – a form of yeast liquid which is rich in alcohol and has a strong flavour – from vat bottoms, and an apprentice brewer called Arthur Jackson.[28] Of these names, those of McMullen, Dockery and Jackson continued well into the twentieth century through the employment of various family members.

3

THE DAWN OF A NEW CENTURY

The turn of the twentieth century saw significant cultural changes for Ireland. Queen Victoria was continuing her reign – which was to be the longest in British history. Technology was bringing new developments that would change the course of social history irrevocably: a strange horseless carriage was seen on the streets of the cities of the British Empire. In Dublin, however, social change still had a long way to go.

CONDITIONS IN DUBLIN IN 1900

In 1900, social conditions in Dublin were in decline. When the Act of Union took effect in 1801, many members of the aristocracy had returned to Britain or to their country estates and had abandoned their houses in Dublin. The Liberties houses had, over time, become tenements housing the poor. One house, No. 5 South Earl Street, which had originally been built for a single family, in 1900 was home to eleven families, consisting of fifty-one people. The families shared a single toilet and one water tap in the backyard.[29]

The Famine of the 1840s had led to large-scale migration from the rural areas of Ireland to the cities, particularly Dublin, by people in search of employment. Some arrived in Dublin hoping to emigrate from Dublin port but found that they could proceed no further:

The city was packed, especially with destitute women and children, widowed, orphaned, abandoned or left behind as the menfolk sought work in England. The large number of soldiers barracked in Dublin, and the high proportion of Irish soldiers in the British Army, brought its own problems: numbers of women, both married and unmarried, and their children, were left to fend for themselves when the soldiers were moved on, or returned to Dublin on the death or desertion of their soldier husbands.[30]

Figures show that 42.2 percent of the population of Dublin were described as being in 'general service' – having no particular trade or profession – and, as such, were living around or below the poverty line. If those in the workhouse are included, this figure rises to about 44 percent.

The poverty line – the amount of money required each week for subsistence – was defined by Seebohm Rowntree in York[31] and modified by Lumsden for Dublin conditions in 1905 as follows:

One Man	7s 0d
One Woman	7s 0d
Man and Wife	11s 8d
Man, Wife and one Child	14s 6d
Man, Wife and two Children	18s 10d
Man, Wife and three Children	21s 8d
Man, Wife and four Children	26s 0d[32]

An illustration of poverty in Dublin at this time is given by Sir Charles Cameron (Chief Medical Officer of Dublin Corporation) in his *Reminiscences:* he gives examples of Dublin families of six people living on sixteen shillings a week in 1911, a family of seven living on fourteen shillings a week, and a family of five living on ten shillings a week. He estimated that many thousands of families had weekly incomes of no more than fifteen shillings[33] and that 33.9 percent of all families in Dublin lived in a single room.[34]

Along with the misery associated with living in poverty and in cramped conditions, there was the inevitable problem of disease. In the nineteenth century, Dublin had the unenviable record of having the highest rate of contagious diseases in Europe. In 1881, when Sir Charles Cameron was appointed Chief Medical Officer for Dublin Corporation, the city also had the highest death rate in Europe.[35]

Overcrowding was the most significant cause of the spread of disease throughout Dublin. Most diseases were spread through respiratory problems and bodily contact, which occurred when a family or group of people lived and slept in one room. Beds were often non-existent, and whole families slept on straw, which was never thrown out or replenished. What passed for bed coverings were generally old rags, and so the bacteria responsible for the diseases remained in constant contact with the people sleeping in the room.

When a person died, from whatever cause, he or she was waked in the family room. This custom, which was part of the culture of Irish people, often entailed three or four nights of 'waking'. Apart from the enormous cost of supplying food, beer, poitín and tobacco to the visitors, the wake often spread the disease from which the victim had died to many of the visitors. Then, even for the poorest Dublin family, a four-horse hearse constituted a show of respectability to the community – despite the fact that the family had to borrow heavily from moneylenders to finance the show.[36]

In the latter half of the nineteenth century, many initiatives were launched by Sir Charles Cameron and Dublin Corporation to counteract the ravages of the various diseases that were then prevalent. Among others. the Public Health Committee, Paving Committee and Sanitary Committee aimed to improve the sanitary lot of Dubliners. Dublin had two 'fever hospitals' – one at Cork Street, the other at North King Street. When a person died of a fever, the house was cleaned and disinfected – something that was seen as a sign of shame amongst Dubliners.

Streets, alleys and courts were washed by washcarts. As these washcarts drew their water from the Liffey, itself an open sewer, much of the infection was redistributed around the streets.[37] Dublin Corporation set up its own cleansing depot in Marrowbone Lane in 1865 for the cleaning and disinfecting of clothes and bedding.

The concerns of Sir Charles Cameron are visible in a public-health report on 'The Causes of Deaths in the City of Dublin in 1900'. The most prevalent diseases reported are smallpox, measles, scarlet fever, typhus fever, whooping cough, diarrhoea, dysentery, typhoid fever and phthisis.[38] Although a smallpox epidemic in 1895 claimed one life a day in Dublin,[39] it was phthisis, later categorised as tuberculosis, which was to be the greatest challenge for the population of Dublin in the following half-century.

GUINNESS FAMILIES IN DUBLIN IN 1900

The Guinness company, being loyal to the Crown, gave each labourer an extra week's wages to mark the Queen's Diamond Jubilee in 1897. The managers and brewers received an extra month's salary. The first week of April 1900 saw the visit of Queen Victoria to Dublin. The visit was organised principally by the merchants of the city, who had appointed a planning committee headed by Alex Findlater. Guinness had already committed five hundred guineas to the erection of a stand on the north side of the Liffey, opposite the Guinness jetty, from which the employees could cheer the Queen on her way to the Vice-regal Lodge in the Phoenix Park.

Less than a year after her visit to Dublin, Queen Victoria died. The Guinness brewery decided to close on Saturday 2 February 1901 'in accordance with the King's Proclamation for the funeral of Her Late Majesty, the Queen'. Some months later, on 23 September 1901, it was decided that from that year on, each employee would be given an extra day's holiday in honour of the Queen, to be known as 'Queen's Day'. Initially, this day was selected by the company; in 1901, the date selected was 6 October.

A year earlier – as an experiment – the company had decided to employ ten female clerks in the bookkeeper's office at a salary of £1 per week. In order to ensure that they were well looked after, one lady, a Miss Hunter, was engaged as Lady Superintendent at £1, 10 shillings a week. By 25 March 1901, a decision had been made to engage another six ladies as 'temporary female clerks' at £1 per week. This arrangement continued until March 1908, when it was decided to hold a competitive examination, after which it was decided to appoint a group of ladies, 'being relatives of employees'.[40]

Two commentators at the start of the century were acutely aware of the struggle facing poor Dublin families. Sir Charles Cameron, Chief Medical Officer of Dublin Corporation, wrote in his Reminiscences:

> During the thirty-two years that I have been the Chief Health Officer of Dublin, I have seen much of life amongst the poor and the very poor, and I have many remembrances of painful scenes that I have witnessed in their miserable homes.[41]

Similarly, the Guinness Chief Medical Officer, Dr John Lumsden, wrote of the importance for Dubliners of making a show of respectability at times like a death in the family. Lumsden wrote in detail about people's need for a three- or four-day wake with plenty of food and drink, followed by a funeral with a four-horse hearse, when a two-horse hearse would have sufficed.[42]

Dr John Lumsden, who had been promoted to Chief Medical Officer in 1899, was an admirer of Dublin Corporation's Chief Medical Officer, Sir Charles Cameron, and had wide-ranging ideas on social reform for Guinness workers. He was well aware of the significance of the moves made by Cameron to inspect houses in the city, as well as dairies, abattoirs and lodging houses. Lumsden knew that Cameron had wide powers to clean up and disinfect such premises and that this had been a significant factor in the struggle against various diseases, particularly tuberculosis.

So, with the full approval of the Guinness board, Dr Lumsden set out on 17 November 1900 to spend two months inspecting the homes of every Guinness employee. In order to gain the approval of the board, Lumsden had written to the managing director, Sir Reginald Guinness, stating: 'It is with a deep sense of duty that I venture to bring under your notice the subject of tuberculosis, its prevention and treatment among your employees and their families.' Lumsden would have been well aware of the description of some Dublin dwellings by Cameron's predecessor, Dr Mapother, as 'fever nests'.

Lumsden's inspection of dwellings was well planned. He notes that 'a considerable time was taken up prior to the inspection in obtaining the necessary information from the various departments as to the correct addresses of the employees.'[43] The employees, therefore, would have had notice of the inspection. In addition, Lumsden had served for six years as the junior medical officer, residing at the company dispensary; his duties would have included seeing most of the employees when they were sick. As the Dispensary was, until 1901, in Thomas Court, in the heart of the tenement houses, he would have had occasion to visit the dwellings when the employee or any member of his family was sick. He would not, therefore, have been a stranger to many of the Guinness families.

In the few cases where he was met with distrust initially, he explained that 'the object of the visitation was purely philanthropic on the part of the firm, and further, that only voluntary information as to [the families'] private lives was sought.'[44] Remarkably, there was only one case where he was denied admission to a dwelling:

> In only one instance did I fail to gain admission to a house, viz., that of a gate porter, who holds strong socialist views – a flat refusal of admission being given to me – not from any personal motive but on the grounds of principle. He held that it was no business of an employer how or where his servant lived. I wasted no words on him, but passed on to the next.

In the appendices of Lumsden's report is a list of the many actions taken as a result of the inspection. In the board reports afterwards, it is noted that certain men were called to account for the state of their houses. At no stage is there any further mention of the gate porter who refused admission; this demonstrates the the strong but narrow focus of the visitations and the ability of Lumsden to accept a principle which was later to become an important part of twentieth-century social reform.

Lumsden states that he visited a total of 1,752 residences, covering the city from Santry to Templeogue and from Clondalkin to Sandycove. The total number of employees visited was 2,287; including dependants, the gross total was 7,343 individuals visited over a two-month period.[45]

The inspection took place from 17 November 1900 to 17 January 1901. Allowing for nine Sundays and three days off at Christmas, Lumsden must have worked a total of forty-eight days, including Saturdays. This gives an average of 36.5 houses visited per day. As the houses concerned would not have had electricity, the inspection would have had to be limited to the hours of daylight – say 8 AM to 4.30 PM, a total of 8.5 hours, it being wintertime. Allowing half an hour for lunch, the inspection would have taken around eight hours per day. So, with 36.5 houses visited per day, this works out at between four and five houses an hour! When you consider the amount of detail in the report, this work has to be seen as a labour of love for the company and the employees.

An important part of the report is Lumsden's classification of the dwellings on the basis of sanitation. Whereas dwellings were classified in the 1841 Census on the basis of the number of walls, rooms and windows, it was not until 1913 that Dublin Corporation began to classify houses on the basis of sanitation.[46]

Lumsden classified dwellings under three headings. His findings relating to the homes of Guinness employees were as follows:

CLASS	SANITATION	PERCENTAGE
One	Adequate	53.4
Two	Fair	20.4
Three	Defective	26.0

He also classified them according to appearance:

APPEARANCE	PERCENTAGE
Satisfactory	76.9
Overcrowding	15.4
Very dirty	13.9

Lumsden then goes on to place the dwellings on a thirteen-stage table, combining the above classifications. He goes to great lengths to record the fact that his decisions were not unduly critical – that he listened to explanations offered by the residents. He says:

> I discovered individual cases, such as small wages and a large family, debt, sickness in the family, family bereavement, etc, before finally adjudicating.[47]

In all, he condemned 35.5 percent of all dwellings as unfit for human habitation and went on to ascribe the following factors as contributing to the production of 'squalid, miserable and unhealthy homes':

> Dirty personal habits, bad management, alcoholism, the existence of a great number of old tenement houses in the neighbourhood of the brewery, occupied by employees.[48]

He then goes on to give reasons for the above classifications, most of which were later outlined by Cameron. In particular, he says in relation to alcoholism:

> For my part, I have always sympathised with the working man in his social surroundings; he has few opportunities of relaxation or enjoyment outside of the club or public house.[49]

These words were to be echoed twelve years later by Cameron.[50] Lumsden reserves his harshest criticism for the conditions of the tenement houses, occupied by 24.2 percent of Guinness employees. The houses, he said, are 'dens of disease . . . so impregnated with filth and so utterly rotten that they should be regarded as unfit for human habitation.'[51] He refers to the decaying vegetable matter, the solid excrement of children soiling the stairways, the sickening stench, and the inadequacy of the water supply: water had to be carried in jugs and buckets from the yard. That water was then held for twenty-four hours in filthy, disease-ridden rooms before being consumed.

He draws a parallel with the spread of pulmonary tuberculosis and states, as Cameron had done, that the solution was to rehouse the people concerned. He concludes: 'But alas! There is no place to go.'[52]

The lavatory arrangements are also heavily criticised, particularly in the Earl Street area, where there were six toilets for about forty-five families, each family consisting of at least four people:

The females do not use these closets, I was informed, but instead use buckets which they empty into the dustbins. This is a truly shocking state of affairs. . . . [53] The actual closets are deplorable and appallingly filthy . . . the seats often made of common half-inch unplaned deal, put together in the roughest manner. In many cases I found them choked up to six or eight inches above the seat with solid human excrement![54]

On the issue of overcrowding, there was some slightly better news in relation to the Guinness employees. Lumsden found no case in which a brewery family occupied one room in common with another family: 'a not-uncommon state of affairs in the Dublin slums, I regret to say.' There are traces of Victorian morality interspersed with genuine concern, however, when he condemns sixteen named families where grown-up members of the opposite sex slept in the same room: 'This overcrowding, besides being unhealthy in the extreme and a means for the spread of disease, is also highly immoral.' In particular he refers to a particular address in which 'three young men live with an unmarried female.'[55]

Lest the report be seen as completely critical of the living conditions of Guinness employees, it should be noted that Lumsden is generous in his praise for many of the dwellings, and he names the families and their addresses. He says: 'these houses were all clean, tidy and home-like, many of them I am extremely pleased to be able to state were scrupulously clean and, in every sense, a credit to the occupiers.[56]

He produced a table giving marks out of a hundred and recommending that prizes – already agreed with the board – be given to the top five families. In addition, he recommended that a printed certificate of merit be presented to those who achieved in excess of 60 percent.

He summarises his report to the board by saying: 'I consider the conditions under which most of your people live, move and have their being is anything but satisfactory and far from what one would desire.'[57] He continues the theme mentioned earlier that the only solution to this problem is the erection of better housing at a modest rent. He expresses great satisfaction that Dublin Corporation, on the recommendation of Cameron, is giving consideration to such an exercise. Then he turns his attention to the Guinness board, saying:

> If the firm could only see their way to erect more tenement buildings, I am convinced our people would flock to them from the wretched tenement buildings, the mortality returns would be diminished, greater contentment and happiness made possible, less sickness, want and misery would be evident. . . . The moral effect of the inspection has been productive of much good . . . it has shown the people the interest the firm takes in their welfare.[58]

The word 'tenement' at the time referred to a good-quality form of basic housing. With the statement above, Lumsden laid the ground plan for the future of Guinness's munificence to their workers for the first half of the twentieth century.

THE FOLLOW-UP TO LUMSDEN'S INSPECTION

At the end of his report, Lumsden made six suggestions for the consideration of the board of directors of Guinness and for the managing director, Sir Reginald Guinness. He suggested that an inspector of dwellings be appointed, that allowances such as sick pay be withheld from employees who continued to reside in dwellings condemned by the company, that a register be kept of suitable lodgings, that efforts be made to dissuade employees from occupying rooms in old tenement houses, that cooking classes be developed for the women, and that annual certificates of merit be awarded for houses that were kept in an exemplary manner.[59]

50

Appended notes were submitted by Dr Lumsden. He stated that no offence appeared to have been caused by the Medical Officer's visit, that the locality of the workmen's homes appeared to be chiefly determined by the wives, who wished to be near the shops, and that the number of homes showing defects which were irremediable except by considerable structural alterations amounted to 26 percent on the whole.[60]

The board discussed Lumsden's report on 4 April 1901. The directors went through each section of the report in detail. Some of the notes of the meeting were as follows:

Pending the erection of the Corporation's houses on the Bride Street area and the erection of Lord Iveagh's houses on the Bull Alley area, the only practical suggestion would seem to be that Mr Busby (Registry Department) should place himself in touch with the existing agencies for the letting of houses.

Average number of families using the one WC. Dr Lumsden to submit a draft letter to the Public Health Authorities with a view of urging them to take steps in this connection.

Cases of members of the opposite sex occupying the same sleeping apartment. (Particular case mentioned) Dr Lumsden will ascertain whether this case still exists, and if so will communicate with the Parish Priest.

It was decided to give prizes of £1 and a certificate to each of the five persons recommended by Dr Lumsden, and to give certificates to all employees . . . who obtained a percentage of 60 or over.[61]

Following this meeting, in October 1901, there is a record of those who were named in the report as living in unsanitary dwellings being interviewed by a personnel manager (not named).

The first man stated that, since the doctor's visit, his house had improved; the second man stated that he had moved house.

He also said that his wife was a 'bad character', and it was very hard to keep either his house or his children in a proper condition. The third man had found a new house. He also had a wife of bad character. At one time he was separated from her for about a year and a half and that, on her promising to mend her ways, he took her back again – but she was as bad as ever. The fourth man stated that the reason for the staircase being dirty was that his wife had been laid up in bed for the previous five months and had not been able to attend to the cleanliness of the house. The fifth man had no excuse but stated that he thought his house was sufficiently clean, and the sixth man had lately done up his premises, and promised to keep them in better order for the future.[62]

The significance of the follow-up was that it showed the determination of the company, within the good offices of Dr Lumsden, to show its workers that, despite the discomfort of the reprimands and the lame excuses, the company cared for their well-being, their health and their future.

OTHER INITIATIVES OF LUMSDEN

Lumsden and Cameron also shared an interest in nutrition. In about 1911, Cameron drew up a table comparing living conditions in Dublin families, their income, their diet, and therefore the nutritional value they gained.[63] Lumsden had preceded him with a similar study in 1903.

Lumsden firstly issued leaflets to nursing mothers in Guinness families on the importance of the proper nourishment of babies and children. While advocating the breast-feeding of infants, he warned about the cleanliness of utensils and the relative lack of nourishment in tinned milk, then popular in Dublin city, because it was condensed from skimmed milk.

Later, in 1903, he prevailed on seventeen women, who were wives of Guinness workers and also mothers, to keep diaries of the family income and expenditure. This is a fascinating study of how the household income at the time was spent on food, fuel, rent and other discretionary items. One such example for a nine-week period showed an income of £16, 11 shillings. The expenditure is carefully detailed to the nearest penny.[64]

Food came to £10, 5 shillings and sixpence. The rest is spent on rent (£1–16–0), oil and gas, coal and coke, soap, Burial Society (popularly known as the 'Bury Yourself Society'!), clothing, boots, tobacco and matches (twopence) debts paid off, sundries, and an amount 'kept back by husband' (£1–6–6). Each item of food purchased every day is specified, as is twopence 'chapel money' on Sunday and threepence for children's pocket money.

Lumsden goes into great detail on this study. He looks at food values, at the amount of protein purchased and consumed, and at carbohydrates. For example, he states that, at one penny, an egg is bad value for the amount of nourishment it provides. He also uses the study to look at housing and overcrowding:

> Most of our men like to be near their work, and the wives close to the shops, the result being a large number of our people reside in old tenement houses, most of which are dens of disease and are both overcrowded and unsanitary.

There was also in existence at the time a co-op Brewery Store where families were given a discount of 10 percent. Most men were given working clothes and boots by the company and also wore these in their leisure time. 'Good clothes' were almost always reserved for going to church on Sundays. Many will remember the old nursery rhyme of the time:

> *Janey Mac, me shirt is black, what'll I do for Sunday?*
> *Get into bed, and cover your head, and don't get up till Monday!*

Lumsden also tells us that the average income of a Brewery family was 24 shillings and threepence. In many cases, this was supplemented by the women doing charring, washing, nursing or dressmaking work. We have already seen how Edward Cecil Guinness gave employment to the daughters of Guinness workers in the Kingsbridge Mills. Lumsden's study also tells us that, in 1903, the children, mainly daughters, of Guinness workers were employed by well-known Quaker firms, such as Goodbody's tobacco factory, Jacobs biscuit factory and Pims clothing factory.

In his efforts to better the lot of the Guinness family, Lumsden refers to lack of education as a major obstacle. He states:

> I personally have always found the majority of our men and their wives reasonable, intelligent and anxious to learn. They have to be tactfully handled and kindly treated, but they are always respectful, apparently grateful, and often quick in appreciating the necessity for improvement. There are, of course, many infirmities of national character which time and education can alone overcome; but I am sanguine of the results, and I believe our people are capable of improvement, and worthy of the effort.

Lumsden concludes this far-reaching report with nine suggestions – all of which were to influence the social life of Guinness families for the following forty years. These were:

1 Encouragement of technical education amongst the younger generation

2 Popular lectures of an educational description

3 Encouragement of healthy out-of-doors sports, athletic exercise and gymnastics among the men and boys

4   The distribution of literature dealing with hygiene and the prevention of disease

5   Practical demonstrations in cooking to the mothers and young women

6   Distribution of pamphlets dealing with infant feeding

7   Giving opportunities for recreation to the men and their wives, in the shape of concerts or social evenings during the winter months

8   Encourage a closer intercourse between the higher officials and the labouring men after working hours

9   The housing issue

This final point is described as being the most important of all. Lumsden expands on the point by stating:

> Until our families are given the opportunity of being comfortably and decently housed, we cannot expect to do much in raising their social and moral standard. I therefore make so bold as to look forward to the day when a Brewery Model Village is built on the lines of Cadbury's at Bournville, and Lever Brothers at Port Sunlight, where our people can obtain a small one- or two-storeyed cottage at reasonable rent.[65]

Looking back, a hundred years later, at the social progress made by Guinness workers and their families, one can easily recognise the structures that were put in place, based on the above suggestions made by this remarkable man.

LUMSDEN'S RESEARCH ON HOUSING

Lumsden undertook, in 1905, a detailed study tour of the health spas of Germany and Switzerland, followed by a study of the two model villages of Bournville and Port Sunlight. He coyly entitled this report: 'A Summer Ramble'.[66]

The houses at Bournville were built by the Cadbury family when they moved their factory from the slums of Birmingham to a green-field site southwest of the city in an area through which the River Bourne flowed. Initially, Cadburys negotiated cheap fares on the railway to enable their workers to go to work. At the same time, they commenced a building programme of good-value housing in the form of a village with various social facilities. In due course, they were able to house most of their workers in clean and healthy surroundings, thereby increasing life expectancy and improving their health.

Port Sunlight was built on similar lines at Birkenhead, on Merseyside, by Mr Lever for the workers in his soap factory. Lever had started life as a grocer in Bolton and, having built up a successful business, started to manufacture soap. As he built his factory, he also began building houses, thus improving the social conditions and the health of his workers.

When John Lumsden visited these villages in 1905, Bournville had been ten years in existence and Port Sunlight had been there for sixteen years. In order to achieve a full inspection, he had brought along letters of introduction from Sir Charles Cameron, Chief Medical Officer of Dublin Corporation. Lumsden was highly impressed with both villages. The five hundred houses in Bournville offered clean accomodation and hot and cold running water, and Lumsden was most taken with the support structure that existed there. He found well-laid-out gardens, playgrounds, schools, tennis grounds, football pitches, a gymnasium, and a swimming pool. He also found a well-run Athletic Union, separate physical-culture drill for boys and youths, and two social clubs, with a library, reading room and billiard room.

Port Sunlight offered similar amenities. There were about six hundred houses, with tree-lined avenues and pleasant lawns. He found two general Refreshment Halls, one for the men, and one for the women and girls. One hall had been opened in 1891 by

Gladstone, and bore his name. This building doubled as a concert hall, and could hold a thousand people.

In relation to the women's hall, Lumsden gives examples of the extent and value of the food being served. There was an open-air auditorium, and a social club with reading, smoking and billiard rooms. There was also a bowling green. He was very impressed with the Technical Institute, which had a wide-ranging syllabus, covering languages, science subjects, dressmaking, shorthand and typing, and engineering. He also outlined all the many clubs that existed in Port Sunlight, as well as the comprehensive sports facilities and Athletic Union.

In the following decade, partly as a result of what he had seen at Bournville and Port Sunlight, Dr Lumsden introduced, or was instrumental in the introduction of, many new initiatives. These included cookery and nutrition classes for women evening concerts in the Workmen's Rooms at Bellevue (also, later, spelt 'Belview') for women, technical education for boys and young men, the first Irish branch of the St John Ambulance Brigade, the purchase of a number of beds at the Royal Hospital for Consumptives at Newcastle, County Wicklow, for the exclusive use by Guinness employees and their families,[67] physical exercises for boys and young men, swimming lessons for boys at the Iveagh Baths, the installation of a gymnasium at St James's Gate in 1905, which led directly to the founding of the St James's Gate Brewery Athletic and Cycling Union.[68]

4

Guinness Social Initiatives

in the Twentieth Century

Queen's Day[69]

Queen's Day originated in the celebrations to mark the visit of Queen Victoria to Dublin in April 1900, and the first Queen's Day took place on 6 October 1901. By 1909, Queen's Day had moved to June; by that time it consisted of a lavish entertainment at the grounds of the RDS (Royal Dublin Society) at Ballsbridge in Dublin. The entertainment took the form of a fête, consisting of fun-fair items, several bands, and various tents where food and drink was served.

As the RDS grounds are about four miles south of the city centre, and most Guinness families lived within half a mile of the Brewery in the inner city, transport to Ballsbridge had to be arranged. At the time, Dublin and its suburbs were blessed with a good tramway system, so trams were laid on from three separate locations. The first was from outside the Brewery at 'the Fountain', located at the junction of James's Street and Steevens Lane, the second was from Dolphin's Barn on the South Circular Road, and the third was from Hanlon's Corner on the North Circular Road.

In 1909, the company issued 13,675 tickets in total to the fête. The tickets entitled the holders to free beer and sandwiches, with the children getting vouchers for soft drinks and rides on the amusements. A number of complications arose over the years, however, mainly to do with tickets being transferred. As a result, a small number of men acquired enough vouchers to get very drunk, and they became boisterous on the trams. In most cases, this appeared to have occurred when men demanded the beer dockets from their wives and from the growing number of teetotallers in their number.

At that time in Dublin, there was a resurgence of nationalism, and the labour movement and religious fervour were growing. A society for non-drinkers had been formed in 1875, after an Irish bishops' pastoral letter around the Gospel narrative of Jesus on the Cross, when Christ said: 'I thirst.' The society was called 'The Confraternity of the Sacred Thirst of Jesus'.[70] A number of its members objected strenuously to their work colleagues getting very drunk and wrote to the manager of the Cooperage Department, Mr L. A. Witz, suggesting that the women's tickets be exchanged for chocolates only, and the men to have a choice of beer or cigarettes. Despite these problems, the fête continued to be popular. It was not held in 1915 due to the Great War, and following the war it was abandoned completely.

The Queen's Day concept remained right up to the 1960s. The company fête, known as the Fanciers' Show (discussed in Chapter 5 below), held in the Iveagh Grounds in summertime, included entertainment and games for children, as well as being a craft fair. This later became the Guinness Family Day. One day of an employee's annual leave was still called 'Queen's Day' up to the 1960s.

During its term, the main suppliers of services to the company for Queen's Day were the Dublin United Tramway Company, the Dublin Metropolitan Police, the Royal Dublin Society, the Royal Irish Constabulary Band and the Royal Scots Fusiliers. On 17 June 1914, those attending the event consumed 26,500 ham sandwiches, 25,000 pints of stout, 21,000 buns, 9,000 biscuits and 30,000 cups of tea!

The first reference to an annual entertainment is to a 1906 entertainment in the Workmen's Rooms in Belview, which cost £88, 6 shillings and sixpence.[71] Earlier that year, there had been a proposal for a 'smoking concert', which was to include the serving of alcoholic drinks. Although this proposal was deemed unacceptable, a concert did take place, without, one assumes, any alcoholic drink. Later, the company arranged an entertainment to commence on 28 October 1907, with a budget of £90.

These concerts continued in the Workmen's Rooms until 1928. Later, they transferred to the Olympia Theatre (and other locations, including the Father Matthew Hall) on Sundays and subsequently to the Mansion House.

I have fond memories of falling in love for the first time when, at five years of age, the young daughter of a Brewery electrician was presented on stage in the Mansion House in the 1940s. As the curtains opened, this delightful young lady was seen swinging on a wooden star to the playing by the band of the latest Frank Sinatra hit, 'Would You Like to Swing on a Star?' All these concerts had an MC, who was a Brewery man and member of the entertainment committee by day and, by night, a dickie-bowed impresario introducing each act. In this particular instance, the man concerned was Harry Carrick (supervisor of the Cooperage Time Office), who, on cracking a joke, produced a wet hankie from his pocket, wiped his eyes and wrung out the wet hankie on top of the band in the orchestra pit!

When the Rupert Guinness Hall opened in 1951, the concerts transferred there, with the first one being held in the hall in January 1953. The role of MC was taken over by Paddy O'Brien (supervisor of the Administrative Department Time Office), who looked resplendent in a white dinner jacket and appeared on stage with heavy eye make-up and red lipstick. The phenomenon of television had just arrived in Ireland, and one of the many imported American programmes of the time was *The Jack Benny*

Show; it was on this style that Paddy O'Brien based his MC-ing of the concerts.

Tickets to the Guinness concerts were like gold dust. The shows ran for six nights a week for four weeks, and there was a different-coloured ticket for each night. The tickets were printed on cardboard measuring about three inches by two inches, with a letter of the alphabet in the top right-hand corner. This was because most of the colours were repeated over the course of the four weeks. Most importantly, the tickets carried two dreaded warnings: 'NOT TRANSFERABLE' and 'CHILDREN IN ARMS NOT ADMITTED'.

Whatever about the children in arms, many of the tickets *were* transferred. Indeed, most working-class Dublin children appeared to get in to the Guinness concert. Of course, the tickets were considered great value since they were free, although, in the case of non-Guinness families, favours may have been called in!

Each night, there was a packed house. Inside the auditorium, burly stewards made room for everyone. Seating was mixed, with a small number of individual seats and a lot of benches. The trick was to get seated on an individual seat: if you were put on the benches, which were made of shiny leatherette, the stewards just pushed more people in until someone fell off the far end. Up on the balcony, there were no benches, only seats, so if you were someone of importance, such as a manager or a foreman, you got to go there.

THE MEDICAL DEPARTMENT

To a non-Guinness person, the term 'Medical Department' might conjure up images of a small consulting room on the company premises in which a doctor sees employees on a twice- or three-times-weekly basis. In the Guinness company, however, it was much more than this. Guinness's tradition of philanthropy and generosity was later formalised in 1888, by which time the

Guinness workers and their dependants were cared for, from womb to tomb.

Officially, during the nineteenth century, workers were considered the virtual chattels of their employers, to be used and discarded at will. There was no allowance for sickness, and certainly no retirement schemes. Men and women started work as soon as they were physically able to do so, and continued with the company until they died or had to leave their employment due to sickness. There was no state social welfare system, so those who were unable to earn a living had to enter the state workhouses or live off the generosity of their neighbours. While this might have been possible in rural areas where people could grow their own food, it was not possible in the cities.

There were, however, some employers of conscience who believed in the principle of *noblesse oblige*. Notably, the Quaker employers in Britain – the Cadburys, Rowntrees, Terrys, Frys and Levers – cared for their employees and did what they could to ensure that their lot was improved. This was done on the basis that happy and well-fed labourers generally worked better and were more likely to respect each other and their employers.

This principle came naturally to the Guinness family. As well as being resourceful and good businessmen, they were deeply religious. They believed that wealth was a gift from God and, as such, was to be shared with those who had helped them achieve it. They also made sure that sufficient resources were reinvested in the business. In most cases, before incorporation the philanthropy of the Guinness family was on an informal rather than a formal basis.

Sir John Lumsden wrote, when looking back in 1944 over his fifty years in the Medical Department, that, when he joined the company in 1894, he had met many old employees who spoke warmly of the generosity of 'Mr Cecil' and 'Sir Edward'.

Lumsden refers to a report submitted to Mr John T. Purser in 1881 by the two medical officers which stated that attendances at the Dispensary in 1880 amounted to 19,000 persons and that 2,206 sick people had been visited. Forty-four percent of the deaths at the time were due to pulmonary tuberculosis. Other deaths in that year were due to smallpox, typhus and typhoid. The medication prescribed that year included 764 bottles of wine, 535 bottles of whiskey and 213 bottles of brandy![72]

Medical officers had been appointed since 1869 and, from 1879, pensions were paid to widows and orphans. The staff of the Medical Department were housed in Belview Buildings from about 1870, and this arrangement continued until a new, purpose-built Medical Department was built in Robert Street in 1901. In line with the prvision of primary care for the Guinness employees, there were strong formal links, internally, at the time with the Co-op Store and the Registry Department.

It was from the Belview Buildings Medical Department that the young Dr John Lumsden set out on his historic inspection of employee dwellings in November 1900. On the conclusion of the inspection, the junior doctor in the Medical Department, Dr Copley, was awarded an additional £20 to compensate him for the extra duties he had undertaken during Dr Lumsden's absence.

In 1901, the new purpose-built Medical Department opened its doors on the extreme southern boundaries of the Brewery site at Robert Street. The new department was beside the Stable Yard and across the road from the Grand Canal basin, into which the barges sailed through the lifting Rupee Bridge (so called because the Grand Canal Harbour had been inherited by a Colonel Hutchinson, who then lived in India).[73] The buildings consisted of consulting rooms, waiting rooms, examination rooms, a pharmacy, and offices. Of particular significance was the upper storey, which was designed as accommodation for the resident medical officer. The building also included a huge underground cellar that had various rooms in which equipment and pharmacy materials were stored.

To its many clients or patients, the building became known simply as 'the Dispensary'. There was easy access to it for the workers through Robert Street and the Back Gate. For the families, there was access from Marrowbone Lane into Robert

Street. In order to enable the large number of men working in the Lower Level, the Cooperage, the Racking Shed, the Traffic Department and the Cookes Lane Maltings to access medical services promptly, in later years a small dispensary, known as the Victoria Quay Dispensary, was erected at the east end of the Racking Shed. In 1915, the Robert Street Dispensary was expanded to include a Dental Department and, in 1917, a massage and remedial-exercise section – which was later further expanded to include a physiotherapy clinic.

For seventy years, the Dispensary served the entire Brewery community: workers and their families. When employment in the Brewery was at its height of more than five thousand workers, during the 1950s, this meant a total of approximately twenty thousand people – if pensioners, their dependants, the workers and their families, and the Brewery 'orphans' are included. (The Brewery 'orphans' included people of all ages whose relatives had, at one stage, worked in the Brewery and who were, for whatever reason, incapable of earning a living for themselves.)

The Dispensary acted as a conduit for the dispensing of Guinness benevolence to those people on the margins of society who were in need of care, either physical, emotional or mental. The Dispensary, through the work of the Chief Medical Officer and the 'Lady Visitor', were the outward expression of the benevolence of Guinness. The post of Lady Visitor began in 1879;[74] this person reported on deserving cases to the Chief Medical Officer, who, in turn, either agreed a course of action or sought direction from the board of directors. For example, in the case of the death of a Guinness worker, a visit was made by the Lady Visitor and a report was sent to the Chief Medical Officer. Where the widow was a young woman with children, an offer of employment as an office cleaner was made, with the agreement of the Registry Department.

When employment in Guinnesses was at its peak, the Robert Street Dispensary was a thriving department. From early morning its benches, well-shined by generations of bottoms, were full. If you were at work, you had to get a docket from your foreman

Sir John Lumsden with the staff of the Medical Department, c.1940

(Courtesy Guinness Archive)

Back Row   E. Molloy, P. Connell, A. Stafford, L. Moore, M. O'Sullivan, P. Cumpole, G. Power, P. Murphy.
4th Row   D. Doyle, G. Shepperd, W. Hammond, P. McEnroe, J. Blackford, W. Clarkson, W. Owens, F. Nolan, T. Sheehan, M. Coleman, J. A. Byrne, A. Kavanagh, M. Weir.
3rd Row   R. Halligan, E. Reynolds, J. Davis, A. Edmonds, C. Thomas, R. Blake, B. Bowden, P. Cosgrave, J. Clarke, F. O'Reilly, J. Fleming, P. Fitzpatrick, J. Dalgarno.
2nd Row   S. Byrne, A. Moran, P. Graham, W. Mullen, M. Boylan, M. Lawler, W. Feaney, F. Finn, M. Ecock, M. Kavanagh, F. Power, W. Keogh, B. Butler, A. O'Brien, J. Moore, S. Purcell.
Front Row   R. T. Mahon, Miss D. Roe, M. McDermott, Dr. J. E. Molvey, B. T. Foreman, R. A. Aitken, Miss D. M. Squires, Dr. H. S. Corran, L. Corcoran, M. Corcoran, C. Henry, V. Cranley, C. F. Parkinson, J. Hudson, J. P. Hogan.
On Floor   R. O'Connor, D. Hanks, R. Reid, T. Halpin, J. Mullins, J. Tinklon, J. McGreal, D. Martin, A. Corcoran.

The staff of the Brewery Laboratory in 1958
(The author is seated in the front row on the extreme right)

A drayman enjoys a pint at the 'Tap', c. 1930

BEFORE . . . Slums in the Patrick Street area, before the Iveagh Trust development
(Courtesy Guinness Archive)

AND AFTER . . . The new Iveagh Trust Buildings, Kevin Street
(Courtesy Guinness Archive)

Cookery classes in 'the Beano', Iveagh Trust
(Courtesy Guinness Archive)

Children's playtime at the Beano

(Courtesy Guinness Archive)

Children entering the Beano

(Courtesy Guinness Archive)

Children's mealtime in the Beano

(Courtesy Guinness Archive)

ST. JAMES'S GATE A.F.C.
Winners Irish Intermediate Cup and Leinster Senior League, 1910-11.
Back Row—M. M'Tunnell, J. M'Donald, W. Cleary.
Second Row—T. Keogh (Hon. Secretary); M. Carroll (Chairman); P. Glennon, J. Boylan, H. Litton, G. Reeves, J. Feew, R. M'Donald (Hon. Treasurer
Front Row—J. Ledwidge, J. Owens, J. Donnelly, Dr. Lumsden (President); M. M'Grath (Captain); P. Halpin, F. Marshall.
Sitting—J. Hassan (Vice-Captain).   J. Cleary.

The Guiness Athletic Union football team, 1910–11 season
(Courtesy Guinness Archive)

Playtime at Queen's Day, c. 1910

(Courtesy Guinness Archive)

The first committee of the Guinness Drama Group, April 1949
From left: Ken Brayden, Pauline Monaghan, Audrey Braca, June Learmont
and Jack Bolger

(Courtesy Yvonne Robins)

Rialto Buildings, built for Guinness workers c. 1880

(Courtesy Guinness Archive)

A group of Guinness electricians at a social in the 1950s

Bonny Baby Competition Sir John Lumsden (centre, in top hat) with mothers and babies at the Guinness Medical Department, c.1910

(Courtesy Guinness Archive)

Consulting Room, Medical Department, c.1940
(Courtesy Guinness Archive)

Achieving ISO 9002 in 1992
From left: John McMahon, the author and Vinny Murphy

Belview dining room, c. 1940s

(Courtesy Guinness Archive)

Guinness bowling team, c. 1940

(Courtesy Guinness Archive)

Children's race, Queen's Day at the RDS

(Courtesy Guinness Archive)

Staff of the Brewhouse Time Office c. 1945
Paddy Corcoran (the author's father) is second from the left

Backstage at the Guinness Concert, 1956
From left: Mick Corcoran, Martin Murphy, Ned Poynton, Dick Murphy, Jack Carro
Tommy Murray and Paddy Ennis

Guinness ex-servicemen at the Remembrance Day parade in the 1950s
The parade is led by Nicky Donegan, who manned the Front Gate and was the
tallest-ever Gate Porter at Guinness

Paddy Corcoran and friend at tennis in
the Iveagh Grounds, c. 1940

Trams arriving at the RDS for Queen's Day, c. 1910

(Courtesy Guinness Archive)

No. 2 Staff at the Brewers' Laboratory
From left: Michael Corcoran (the author's uncle), Jim Hudson, Freddie Parkinson, Charlie Hoey and Reg Corcoran (also the author's uncle)

Thady and Teresa Corcoran, the author's grandparents, in the 1940s

or supervisor giving you permission to leave your job. This docket stated your name, your registry number and the time you left the job. You then queued at a hatch, where you gave your name and number and were handed your record card. These cards were colour-coded, depending on whether you were an employee or a dependant. If you could read the doctor's writing, you could actually read your medical information and, at a push, the medical information of the person on the bench beside you. Some doctors were gruff and left the door of their consulting room open. Then came the magic shout: 'Next!' You raced in, sat in the chair and explained, as quickly, and discreetly as possible, what your ailment was. Then it was a quick scribble on your card, medicine was allocated, advice was given, and you were despatched to the pharmacy for the medicine, making sure that you had your docket signed by the doctor for when you returned to your foreman or supervisor.

There are many folk tales about what people overheard outside the door when particular people were with the doctor. In one case, the doctor was reputed to have shouted at the unfortunate patient: 'I wouldn't put my umbrella where you have put that!' In one particular case, which can be verified, a fourteen-year old laboratory boy, still very innocent, was having problems with painful sinuses. He confided this to his laboratory colleagues, and one of the older boys told him that it was best that he – as a laboratory worker – should use the correct technical term in describing his symptoms to the doctor. Thus it was that the young boy complained to the doctor of 'a pain in his b----' (a body part far removed from the sinuses)! Neither the doctor nor the laboratory supervisor to whom it was reported was amused.

Queuing at the pharmacy had its own hazards. In most cases, the prescription was a bottle of something or other – very often a bottle of iron tonic. To get a full bottle, you had to hand in an empty one, however. If you didn't have an empty, you would be interrogated by the pharmacy assistant as to why this was so. As this again took place in a public area, it was important to be ready

65

with the empty bottle to save face. There was an enterprising woman in the huckster shop across the road – a small, dark, cavernous shop which sold everything from paraffin oil to bread, unpackaged butter and loose milk – who did a thriving business in selling empty bottles for a few pence. No one asked how she came by the bottles.

As with most other Guinness departments, your rank within the organisation dictated how you were treated at the Dispensary. Foremen and supervisors, as well as all management grades, could enter the Robert Street building by a different door, where there was a specific queuing area and, furthermore, you could choose which doctor you saw. There was also no need to queue for medicines, as these would be delivered to your place of work by boy messengers.

In 1971, after seventy years of service to the Guinness community, the dispensary at Robert Street was closed and the then formally named Medical Department was moved to a new purpose-built building in James's Street. The Robert Street building was turned into a Training Centre, where it served another twenty-nine years, becoming in 1994 'The Learning Centre'. The original wall plaque stating 'St James's Gate Dispensary 1901' remained in place as the building changed from a place of healing to a place of learning. In 2000, the Learning Centre was transferred to the Guinness Storehouse, becoming part of the Visitors' Centre.

The Battle Against Tuberculosis

From the mid-nineteenth century, Dublin became a city of overcrowded tenement houses described as 'fever nests'. Much work was done by the Dublin Corporation Public Health Department under, firstly, Dr Edward Mapother, and later, Sir Charles Cameron, to rid Dublin of its reputation of having the highest mortality rate in the British Empire, with statistics similar to those of Calcutta.[75] It was against this background that the Guinness Chief Medical Officer, Dr John Lumsden, undertook his inspection of employees' houses in 1900.

In the days long before slogans, Lumsden had notices printed in enamel and posted all over the Brewery premises saying: 'TO PREVENT CONSUMPTION, PLEASE DO NOT SPIT'. He was well aware that spitting was unhygienic and, through the Dispensary, he introduced the use of the Deitweillers pocket flask, which sufferers could spit into and then return to the Dispensary for cleaning and sterilising.

Lumsden was also an advocate of proper living conditions, hygiene, proper nourishment and fresh air to ensure healthy living. As we have seen, he was instrumental in the establishment of the Royal Hospital for Consumptives at Newcastle, County Wicklow.[76] Initially, with the approval of the Guinness Board, he purchased two beds in the hospital for the sole use of Guinness employees, and he later purchased two more beds for the relatives of Guinness workers. This was in addition to the many national sanatoria around Dublin and throughout the country to which Guinness patients were sent – all paid for by the company.

Thankfully, apart from a blip in the statistics in the years 1915 to 1917, during World War I, the incidence of tuberculosis in Guinness workers and among Dublin people gradually lessened throughout the twentieth century. This was due to a combination of better living conditions, improved nutrition and hygiene, and in particular, the prevention of the disease through the Mass X-Ray system introduced in the 1940s.

THE ST JOHN AMBULANCE BRIGADE

The establishment of the St John Ambulance Brigade at St James's Gate came about through a number of initiatives implemented by Dr John Lumsden. Dr Lumsden, who was always interested in physical education for young men and had a good knowledge of first aid, sought to run first-aid classes at the Brewery under the auspices of the Brigade, of which he had been a member in England. Consequently, in 1904 his class of forty members became registered as a division of the Brigade in London. In 1906, the Brigade was established in Ireland, with the formation of other Irish divisions, and Lumsden became the organisation's Commissioner for Ireland. Later, in 1918, in recognition of his work with the Brigade, Dr Lumsden was made a KBE (Knight of the British Empire) and became Sir John Lumsden.

Meanwhile, the St James's Gate Division of the Brigade became part of the Irish Division. The Irish Division had first come to prominence during the 1907 International Trade Exhibition in Dublin and later saw active service during the General Strike of 1913, when it was praised for its impartiality in treating both strikers and police casualties. When the Great War started, more than a hundred men from the St James's Gate Division joined the British Army, the Home Hospital Reserve and the Auxiliary Royal Naval Sick Berth Reserve. The division also saw service in the Rising of 1916 and the Civil War of 1921, having manned posts in the Four Courts and the Gresham Hotel.[77] It was active in giving first aid to the Sherwood Foresters who were ambushed at Northumberland Road during the Rising.

Later, throughout the Brewery, first-aid posts were set up to give first aid on the spot, prior to casualties being brought to the Dispensary. These first aiders were, of course, trained and regularly examined by the St John Ambulance Brigade. Those trained in first aid included the infamous 'jacks clerks', also known as 'latrine timekeepers'. These men, linked to the Times Offices, had the job of sitting in small, draughty offices in the lavatories around the Brewery site. As each 'customer' arrived, he was expected to call out his pay number in exchange for two sheets of coarse lavatory paper. The clerks then noted how long that person spent in the closet; this information was, in due course, reported back to the Time Office. Part of their duty was to be present in case someone was genuinely unwell – for whatever reason – and required first aid!

THE GREAT WAR AND 1916[78]

On the outbreak of the Great War in 1914, many Irish people were loyal to the Crown and volunteered for service in the British Army. In many cases, there was an organised mustering of men. In the Royal Irish Constabulary, for example, there was a contingent of a hundred men who volunteered their services to Sir Neville Chamberlain, the Secretary of State for Ireland, at Dublin Castle. These men, when enlisted, formed one of the first Irish Guards regiments.

At St James's Gate, many hundreds volunteered their services 'for king and country': the personnel records abound with entries relating to a particular employee 'to replace one hand gone to war'. Many, unfortunately, did not return, and the company commissioned a Roll of Honour of the names of those who volunteered, with particular mention of those who had died for the cause.

This Roll of Honour was issued in the form of a leather-bound book, with green-and-gold writing, dedicated to 'employees who served in His Majesty's naval, military and air forces, 1914-18'. The purpose of this book was to 'preserve in a suitable form a record of those who gave their services and, in many instances, their lives, for the defence of the Empire at the most perilous and critical period in its history'. To this day, there are many Guinness families who treasure in their homes this volume as a memorial of a grandparent who left their work at St James's Gate to defend the Empire.

*

The Rising of 1916 caused a great deal of confusion at St James's Gate. Those who were committed to the nationalist cause voluntarily left their work and families and joined the barricades at the various posts taken over by Oglaigh na hÉireann at the GPO, at various posts around the city, at Boland's Mill and, more locally, at the South Dublin Union (later St Kevin's Hospital and now St James's Hospital) and Goodbody's tobacco factory in Marrowbone Lane. The reaction of the British Army was swift. Anyone suspected of involvement in the uprising was arrested and taken to the nearby barracks.

Some of those arrested were simply Guinness employees walking home from work, however. A number of men were arrested in Rialto on their way in to the Brewery for the late shift, and imprisoned in Richmond Barracks in Inchicore. There was a case of one man returning to his home in Emerald Square in Cork Street from the early shift. As he passed the tobacco factory in Marrowbone Lane, he saw that it had been taken over by Volunteers, some of whom were his friends. He was invited inside and, he alleges, was then prevented from leaving by his friends. Eventually, the army overcame the Volunteers and he and the others were taken to Richmond Barracks. After interrogation in the barracks, a small number of the men were released. The vast majority of those arrested were deported to internment camps in Wales, such as Frongoch.

The Guinness directors and management took a very clear stance on those employees who had been arrested and who had absented themselves from work because of the Rising: they were dismissed. The only exceptions were those men who were part of the St John Ambulance Brigade, under Dr John Lumsden, and were on active service providing first aid to casualties on both sides.

A later board memo, written by Colonel H. W. Renny Tailyour, the Managing Director of Guinnesses, indicates the scale of what happened. Of the No. 2 staff, two were deported and two had satisfactory explanations for their actions. Of the labourers, one was killed, two were imprisoned, and thirty-six were deported to English prisons.

In hindsight, the decision to sack almost fifty people who were deemed not to have satisfactory explanations for their involvement in the Rising was a harsh one. Most wrote letters of appeal – to no avail. There was widespread support in the city for the re-instatement of these workers. Support came from the coopers' guild, local businessmen, the trade unions, and the licensed vintners association. The company held fast to its decision, however, and none were re-instated.

During the Troubles, the Guinness premises were occupied in part by the British Army. Accommodation was provided in 98 James's Street for officers. Details of meals provided show that 382 meals were given to officers, and 1089 to noncommissioned officers and men. Regiments in occupation at various times include the Fifty Lancers, the Twelfth Lancers, the Welsh Horses Regiment, the London Rough Riders, the King Edward Horse Regiment, the Duke of Lancaster Regiment, the Sherwood Foresters, the Fifth Staffordshire Regiment, the Royal Irish Rifles, the Munster Fusiliers and the Dublin Fusiliers.

The saga of 1916 in St James's Gate would not be complete without telling of the sad occurrence of the deaths of two gentlemen of the Brewery night staff. The King Edward Horses Regiment was in occupation of the top floor of the Robert Street Malt Store. During the night of 28 April 1916, the regiment captain apparently absented himself and, allegedly, left no one in charge. During the night, Mr C. E. Dockery of the night staff set out on his rounds, which included Robert Street. More than an hour later, when he had not returned, his colleague Mr W. J. Rice went to search for him. Although exactly what happened is unclear, both men were shot dead by the soldiers present.[79] (As part of the same unfortunate episode, two officers of the King Edward Horses Regiment, Captain Lucas and Captain Worswick, were also shot.) Following this incident, the Managing Director issued a statement to the newspapers confirming that neither Mr Dockery nor Mr Rice had been in any way associated with the insurrection.

5

THE GUINNESS ATHLETIC UNION

As part of his campaign for better health amongst the Guinness employees, Dr John Lumsden had actively promoted physical education since his appointment in 1894. This led, in 1905, to the founding of the St James's Gate Brewery Athletic and Cycling Union.[80]

There were, of course, no official sports grounds at that stage. The initial activities were football, cycling, tug-of-war and gymnastics. Problems encountered in the early stages included the lack of a suitable playing pitch, and the lack of a gymnasium. Eventually, a gymnasium was built on the Brewery site; it was opened in 1905. Initial administration was provided by Dr Lumsden, who lobbied the Managing Director for a number of indulgences – including leave on Saturdays (the company worked on Saturdays at the time) for those playing away football matches. In July 1905, a request was made for the tug-of-war team to be granted leave to travel to Kilkenny for a competition. The leave was granted – but their pay was docked.[81]

In October 1905, a committee was formed; it was decided that the annual subscription should be threepence for boys and sixpence for men. The members of the first formal committee were J. Lumsden (Chairman), T. F. Barbor, A. Connor, H. M. Farrell, E. Hewitt, W. L. Bowie, J. Crannie, J. A. Frew, J. Oates and L. A. Witz. The honorary instructor was J. Oates, and the honorary secretary was Robert Mahon. It was agreed that the committee would be responsible to the Head Brewer.[82]

The gymnasium, in particular, thrived, and there was a request some time later for 'a shower apparatus' in 1909. Activities on offer included figure marching, bar and dumbbells, Indian clubs, parallel bars, vaulting horse, boxing, wrestling and fencing. There was a proposal in 1907 to form a rifle club, with a practice range in Fitzsimons Yard in the Brewery. This was not allowed initially but was formed some time later. There was strong pressure from Dr Lumsden for swimming lessons for boys to take place in the Iveagh Baths, in the newly built Iveagh Trust buildings. This was arranged with Captain Bonner of the Iveagh Trust; the instructor was Sergeant Case of the Royal Irish Constabulary. There was the small matter of payment, however: regular invoices for £5 were sent to Dr Lumsden at his home address of 4 Fitzwilliam Place.

The first sports day appears to have been held in August 1909 at the First Lock on the Grand Canal. There were twenty-five events, and the entrance fee for each event was threepence. The poster advertising the event signified the growing national-ism by stating that it was printed by *'An Cló Cumann,* on Irish paper with Irish ink'. Each section of the Union had its own notepaper: the secretary of the rifle club was William Johnston, with an address at 23 Rialto Buildings.

From about 1912, Lumsden started campaigning for a dedi-cated Guinness sports grounds. In a memo to the Board, he refers to the then current pitch, which was 'procured at the First Lock Grand Canal from the Dolphins Barn Brick Company at a yearly rent of £50'.[83] In the course of discussions, there were questions from the Board about 'the Gaelic Game'. Lumsden replied that he had not heard of any political connections between the GAA and the nationalist movement. After a long discussion, the Board decided that it was not in a position to give a field.

By November 1921, the Union was on a sound administra-tive footing, with a paid secretary, Mr W. R. Bowie, who received £50 per annum for his services. By October 1922, the Head Brewer, T. B. Case, paid tribute to the efforts of Mr Bowie in increasing the membership of the Union from 670 to 1250. Meanwhile, Mr Bowie made an appeal to the Managing Director, Mr C. E. Sutton, for funds to allow the Union's present activities to be expanded to include tennis, cricket, handball and other sports. There is a pointed reference in this request of 10 October 1922 to a twenty-five-acre site on the Crumlin Road belonging to a Mr Begg which was available for purchase.

Mr Sutton replied to Mr Bowie on 8 June 1923 proposing that the Union 'continue for two years' while some arrangement was worked out. Meanwhile, negotiations continued on the securing of Mr Begg's field. A letter from a solicitor, Mr H. T. Dix, proposed that Mr Begg would accept £5,200 for his field, having refused £5,000 from the Dolphins Barn Brick Company because 'he did not like the idea of having a quarry in front of his house.'[84]

Lumsden had always referred the Board to the benefits of a company sports grounds and had quoted the examples of Cadburys and Levers. The Head Brewer, Mr T. B. Case, did contact Levers for advice on the matter and was referred to a Mr C. S. Mason of the Industrial Society in London, who carried out such surveys. In October 1923, Mr Mason carried out a survey for which the fee to the Industrial Society was £15–15–0. Travelling expenses were £6–9–6 and 'out-of-pocket expenses' £1–10–0. The subsequent report – which included coloured maps of the proposed grounds – while complimentary, referred to the fact that the site was 'some considerable distance from the trams'.[85]

In fact, the final arrangement was that Lord Iveagh (Edward Cecil Guinness) purchased the site and gave it as a personal gift to the Guinness workers. It was announced on 25 January 1926 that Lord Iveagh had appointed certain trustees in whose names he had placed the sum of £20,000 for the purchase of the Iveagh Athletic Ground. Those trustees were named as Sir J. Lumsden, Mr Barker, Mr Crawford, Mr Gage Green, Mr Mulligan, Mr Walter Phillips, Mr J. G. Mann, Mr P Beggin (it was said that 'Beggin is one of the company's most valued employees on the Labour list') and the Lady Superintendent, Miss Maver. The cost of fitting out Begg's field came to almost £20,000.[86]

In the autumn of 1927, before the Iveagh Grounds were officially opened, Lord Iveagh died and the chairmanship of the company passed to his eldest son, Rupert Guinness, who became the Second Earl of Iveagh.

The Iveagh Grounds on the Crumlin Road were officially opened by the new Earl and Countess of Iveagh on Saturday 14 April 1928 at 3 PM: an important event in the social history of Guinness employees. The official invitation refers to the events that took place on that day: interdepartmental football, interdepartmental tug-of-war, tennis – both men's and mixed doubles – a bowling match, and a girls' physical-culture display.

The annual membership subscription for that year was ten shillings. The application forms were blue for members of management staff and pink for employees, who could opt for deduction this amount to be deducted from their wages at one shilling per month for ten months. A bar was installed in January 1929, the Board donated a piano in 1931, and a stand was erected by Smith and Pearson in 1934 at a cost of £898.[87]

In recognition of the great generosity of Edward Cecil Guinness, First Earl of Iveagh, a memorial plaque was erected on the wall at the Front Offices at St James's Gate, and a copy of the plaque was erected in the pavilion at Iveagh Grounds.

Among the many sections of the Guinness Athletic Union, the most famous was the soccer team, which, in order to qualify for the league matches, had to take on professional players. Following this move, the Gate team won the Irish Free State Shield in 1935. Its more famous players included the soccer international Jackie Carey. The folklore of the soccer club includes the story that the barman in the grounds would always have a line of pints of stout ready at the bar for the team to replenish their energies at half-time. Indeed, many have confessed to consuming much more than a pint at half-time!

One of the sporting highlights each year was the interdepartmental soccer tournament for the La Touche Cup – known colloquially as the 'Touchers Cup'. Rivalry between departments was intense, with flags, banners, slogans and taunts being exchanged all over the Brewery. The matches were held in the evening time in spring, and towards the end of the tournament there would be huge attendances, with the crowds filling the grandstand and the bar. On the day of the final there would be little work done on site as the two teams paraded around, gathering followers as they went. Then the next day, the winning team paraded triumphantly, carrying the cup, in taunting fashion, around all the losing departments!

An annual feature of great interest to the Guinness community was the Fanciers' Show. This began in the 1920s, following on from the Queen's Day. The show incorporated competitions in various handcrafts, from baking to knitting, jam-making and marrow-growing. There was even a hotly contested 'cut and style' competition, where the contestants had the opportunity to model their creations. There was also a 'Bonny Baby' competition.

The competitions were held in a series of marquees in the Iveagh Grounds, with very strict judging procedures. The show was moved to the Rupert Guinness Hall in the late 1960s and was discontinued in the 1970s.

In parallel with the Fanciers' Show were sports competitions, including the hundred-yard dash, the three-legged race and the egg-and-spoon race. After the disbandment of the Fanciers' Show, the Union continued to run an Annual Sports Day in the Iveagh Grounds until 1985.

Then, in 1985, the Guinness company sponsored a Family Day in the Iveagh Grounds during the summer. This was a very popular day for all, with sports, entertainments such as a Punch and Judy show, and a demonstration of the skills of the Air Corps helicopter and the police dog unit. The day also incorporated the old reliable Bonny Baby competition. Politicians and celebrities from the worlds of the theatre and sports mingled with the families of Guinness workers to make the Guinness

Family Day a memorable one. Those who organised the day can justifiably boast that their efforts were always appreciated. Even the weather was superb every year! The Family Day was finally disbanded in 1995.

6

THE IVEAGH TRUST

Although it is perhaps not directly related to the social history of Guinness workers in Dublin, the Iveagh Trust deserves mention due to its prominent role in the history of Dublin and its association with the founder of the Trust, Edward Cecil Guinness, the First Earl of Iveagh.

As outlined earlier, the Guinness family played a significant part in society in Victorian Dublin. The family, who were already involved in caring for its workforce, set up housing blocks for the Guinness workers, firstly in Rialto, with the housing being constructed by the Dublin Artisans' Dwelling Company, and later in Belview, on the fringes of the Brewery complex.

After incorporation in 1886, the company ceased to be family-owned, and the head of the family, Edward Cecil Guinness, who was already involved in many philanthropic activities, found himself with a fortune to spare after selling shares to the shareholders. Thus, in 1890, he set up the Guinness Trust with an initial endowment of £250,000. The bulk of this, £200,000, went towards the construction of working-class housing in London, and £50,000 went on housing in Dublin.[88]

Work began immediately on two housing projects in Dublin, one at the junction of Thomas Court and Belview and another at Kevin Street at the south end of St Patrick's Cathedral. The first building project undertaken was the erection of the Thomas Court complex, adjacent to the brewery, on land acquired from Lord Meath, a director of the Dublin Artisans' Dwelling

Company, along with his wife, Lady Meath. The building was undertaken by the DADC and handed over to the Trust in 1892. These buildings were seen as experimental forerunners of later Trust buildings.[89]

At the time, members of the 'Church' Guinness family were involved in charity work in the East End of London. In Dublin, for some years previously, Edward Cecil and his brother, Arthur Edward, had been involved in restoration work at St Patrick's Cathedral. They had also been actively buying up properties around the cathedral, and between it and Christ Church Cathedral. They had been appalled at the living conditions endured by Dubliners in the filthy tenements and dirty alleys and closes which had developed in an unplanned way in the area. Thus, both in the earlier stages and later, Edward Cecil invested much more than the original £50,000 in the Dublin branch of the Guinness Trust.

The moves which had been made by various Guinness family members came to fruition in 1897 when the Guinness brothers and Sir Talbot Power obtained an Act of Parliament to acquire and convert into a park the area between St Patrick's Cathedral and Bull Alley. The three trustees were to meet all expenses. The park, when complete, was to be called St Patrick's Park and was to be vested absolutely in Dublin Corporation for use by the public. The conversion of the area was a mammoth task, involving the rehousing of displaced people in the Guinness Trust houses in Kevin Street and the building of a market in Francis Street for the displaced traders. This market was a huge improvement for the traders, who sold secondhand clothes and rags: among other things, it incorporated a washing and sterilising plant for the clothes. When it was opened in 1906, this market was also handed over to Dublin Corporation.

In 1903, the Dublin operation of the Guinness Trust, which, by then, had buildings at Kevin Street, at Thomas Court and at a site between the two cathedrals, was renamed 'the Iveagh Trust'. The Dublin Improvement (Bull Alley Area) Act 1899 allowed plans to go ahead for the building of what is now a famous Dublin landmark: the set of housing blocks which incorporated the workmen's dwellings, a swimming pool, a lodging house (now known as the 'Iveagh Hostel') and a large building that held a concert hall, reading rooms, classrooms and exhibition rooms. Teachers were employed to teach and instruct the local children in various handcrafts and life skills. The building holding the concert hall became a well-known Dublin institution, affectionately called 'the Beano'. The concert hall was to feature musical instruments for the purpose of teaching the local children an appreciation of music. The use of the buildings was to be on a non-sectarian basis.

After celebrating its one-hundredth birthday in 1990, the Iveagh Trust continues from strength to strength into the twenty-first century. The swimming pool, which had been handed over to Dublin Corporation in the 1950s, later became a private leisure and health centre. The hostel was modernised and continues to be used for its original purpose of providing low-cost accommodation.

THOMAS COURT AND THE BELVIEW BUILDINGS

A set of rules and regulations concerning the 'workmen's dwellings' at Belview and Thomas Court was issued in 20 March 1935.[90] Preference was given to Guinness employees on shift work with variable hours and those liable to be called out on duty with little notice. Amongst those named were fire-brigade men, boatmen and those working in the brewhouse. The rent at the time ranged from three shillings and sixpence to ten shillings a week.

To qualify for accommodation, application had to be made to the Registry Department; qualification was subject to an inspection of the prospective tenant's previous accommodation. The rules detail how often the halls, landings and stairways should be swept and washed. There were fines for the misuse of the water closets, the keeping of poultry, pigs and other animals was prohibited, and the tenants were not allowed to set up shop or sell goods of any kind. There were also rules concerning the riding of bikes and the playing of cards. Under no circumstances could clothes be hung from the windows to dry. All these rules were enforced by watchmen, who were supplied with hats, coats, boots and leggings, and who patrolled the buildings.

One of the many benefits of living in the buildings was access to the bathhouse once a week. It is said that a washing woman was employed there to wash the children of all the residents.

THE IVEAGH GARDENS, CRUMLIN

This was a later initiative of the Iveagh Trust, undertaken in 1925. A site of about thirty acres was purchased in 1926 from A. Guinness, Son and Co. (Dublin) Ltd, adjacent to the Iveagh Grounds. The design of the housing estate was similar to that of the many 'garden estates' which had been built in various parts of England, including at Bourneville near Birmingham. The Iveagh Gardens scheme was completed in 1936: there were 136 houses in total, 52 with four rooms and 84 with five, housing 637 people in total. The overall cost of the development was £134,000.[91]

7

The Brewery in the Forties and Fifties

What was known in Ireland as 'the Emergency' and in the rest of the world as World War II was a significant time for the people of Dublin and the community of Guinness workers. Ireland, as a Free State under a government led by Éamon de Valera, remained neutral throughout the period. Nonetheless, the effects of the war were certainly felt in Ireland, mainly in terms of the need for a mobilised defence force and, especially, in shortages of food and fuel. There were few motor cars on the road, and large numbers of men volunteered to cut peat or turf in the many bogs in the midlands of Ireland. This turf was collected and stored in huge piles in the Phoenix Park in Dublin for national use. The national army collected large groups of men at various meeting points around Dublin and transported them to and from the bogs. Elsewhere, men would cycle many miles to 'save' the turf and, at harvest-time, to 'save' the harvest.

Individual transportation was mostly by bicycle or on foot. One man related how he cycled every second weekend from Dublin to Mountrath, a distance of about seventy miles each way, to visit his family. Others would walk up to thirty miles either to or from Dublin. In the case of rain – a frequent occurrence – shelter was found under the many bushes beside the road. Food and drink could be easily purchased along the route.

Many men from rural Ireland presented themselves at the Registry Department of St James's Gate looking for employment in the famous Guinness Brewery. In the early part of this period, Guinness recruited very few employees, however. Indeed, in 1943, the company made five hundred men redundant due to a problem with barley supplies.[92] One of the busiest Guinness departments at the time was the Experimental Brewery at the junction of Robert Street and Rainsford Street, which was conducting trials to examine the efficiency of various boiling techniques to conserve fuel. Trials were also conducted to examine several malting techniques and means of generating better extracts from the mash.

In Dublin in general, there was little unemployment. This was because men who lost their jobs often simply emigrated to Britain, where there was plentiful employment in the armed forces and in the munitions factories and other industries. The streets around St James's Gate were empty apart from the early-morning rush of cyclists to work, their rush home for 'the dinner', the return to work, and the rush home at five o'clock for tea.

During the 1950s, however, Guinness started recruiting actively for employees. One worker in Dublin, Paddy Skelton, was working as a tailor's apprentice and lodging with an aunt on the South Circular Road when he presented himself at the Registry Department for assessment, which involved filling in a form and being weighed and measured. There was then a wait of some weeks, during which Paddy had a change of heart about his employment in the tailoring world. He left his lodgings one evening and walked through the night to the family farm on the borders of Wicklow and Carlow. The next day he was in the fields picking potatoes when a telegram arrived from Guinness offering him employment. He returned to Dublin and took the job. Until his retirement in the 1980s, he was a popular and charismatic figure at Guinnesses, not only as a worker, but also as a collector of and expert in vintage cars and farm machinery, which hobby he pursued until his death in 2000.

The end of the war in 1945 marked the return to St James's Gate of the many men who had volunteered for service with the British armed forces in 1939. With them came many other former soldiers, who, although they had not previously worked for Guinness, were now seeking employment. Several hundred former army men were taken on in the various departments; these represented a significant group in their own right. Serving in the armed forces had given them a sense of teamwork, and this was characterised by a show of toughness which didn't always endear them to the Guinness workers of the time.

At the same time at St James's Gate there were increased levels of production, further recruitment of workers, and an increase in appointments of foremen and supervisors. All of this led to an uneasy atmosphere at the Brewery as new colleagues joined shift teams and there were occasional personality clashes. This, in turn, led to calls for the unionisation of the workforce – a move which would isolate the supervisory grades. This situation eventually led to the formation, in 1949, of the first trade union for general workers at the Brewery; many talented union leaders emerged over the next few years.

Buildings erected at the Brewery in the 1940s and early 1950s included the Power Station, set in off the road beside 98 James's Street. The Power Station was originally powered by coal, which was stockpiled north of the building on Cookes Lane. A long conveyor belt carried the coal from the pile area into the furnaces of the station. In May 1951, there was a serious incident in which this conveyor belt caught fire and the fire itself was conveyed into the station. Fortunately, the fire was quickly brought under control.

Beside the Power Station, on the corner of James's Street and Watling Street, was the Registry Building, and beside that was a sugar store, which was converted into a company theatre and assembly hall. This building was a lavishly outfitted theatre with five hundred seats, a balcony, an orchestra pit and a thirty-foot-deep stage with full-size flies and wings, a state-of-the-art lighting board and equipment, six dressing rooms with intercommunication equipment, and a comfortable 'green room'. The hall was named the Rupert Guinness Hall, after the then Lord

Iveagh, and was opened to the public by Lord Iveagh on 4 July 1951.

The Rupert Guinness Hall became the showpiece of the Guinness company and was used for many purposes, in particular the Annual Entertainment every January and various musical events. It also became the centre point in later years for the Guinness Choir, the Guinness Players and the Arthur's Team Variety Group. In August 1951, when the Abbey Theatre burned down in central Dublin, the company loaned the Rupert Guinness Hall to the Abbey Theatre Company. Many famous plays from the Abbey repertoire were performed in the hall, until the Abbey was rehoused in the Queens Theatre back in the city centre.

In Ireland in the 1950s, despite crippling unemployment, there was modest economic growth; this applied also to the Guinness Brewery at St James's Gate. Sir Charles Harvey, a retired Brigadier General who took a keen interest in personnel matters, joined the Board of Directors. He issued a memo on 21 November 1951 in which he outlined a vision of good personnel practice.[93] This vision included methods of consultation, taking a personal interest in the men, training new entrants, coaching boys, retraining older men and offering specific courses for foremen.

Plant tours were established for those who had been in their departments for many years and had little knowledge of what went on in other departments, despite the fact that they were in touch with these areas on a daily basis. By 1953, there were also specific tours arranged for foremen, who, by now, saw themselves as a distinct class situated between the men and management. Separate tours were also arranged for ladies staff, although it was specified that the Lady Superintendent, Miss Coulson, would select who could go on these tours.[94]

This period also marked the beginning of Guinness staff attending external training courses. As the Irish Management Institute was then in the process of being formed, many of the external courses took place in Britain, particularly in Cranfield in

Essex. The company covered all costs, even what were called 'out-of-pocket expenses', which for 'gentlemen was £1 per day and for ladies, ten shillings per day'.

Technical education for boys and men, which began in 1901, was now tightly focused. Boys were expected to take technical courses to prepare them for a general education and were enrolled in selected technical schools. For example, boys who worked in the laboratories were expected to attend the Technical School in Kevin Street to study mathematics, physics and chemistry. Fees were paid, time off was given, and prizes were awarded on examinations passed. Most followed this pattern, but there were a few exceptions. In 1948, for instance, a boy called Desmond Carrick asked for permission to attend the National College of Art instead of a technical school. Carrick later became a well-known artist and was elected a member of the Royal Hibernian Academy. Others asked for permission to attend Caffrey's College so that they could prepare for the No. 1 Staff examination. In these cases, permission was granted – on condition that the applicants paid their own fees.

Attendance at evening classes was carefully monitored by the Registry Department. Roll-call details were sent every week to the company by the schools, and those who skipped classes which had been paid for by the company could expect a call to their manager's office to explain their absence.

In the case of those boys who diligently attended Technical School, there were good rewards, however. One young man, on passing seven subjects in the Leaving Certificate examination, was granted £7 per subject, a total of £49, at a time when the weekly wage was between £3 and £5. Another two young men, Tom and Syl, who were assigned duties on the company switchboard, were sent to daytime speech classes in the Royal Academy of Music off Grafton Street, to improve their speaking voices. These two lads were the envy of their contemporaries: the college was mixed, and they could socialise with young ladies before and after class. They told me that they could also stroll on breaks through St Stephen's Green and chat up the young ladies sitting out in the sunshine to practise their newly learned speech techniques!

The Guinness company was also instrumental, along with the Jesuits and the trade-union movement, in the setting up of the National College of Industrial Relations in Ranelagh. In 1956, courses for foremen were also set up, in conjunction with the High School of Commerce in Rathmines, on 'Training Within Industry'.

On the occasion of the Golden Wedding of Lord and Lady Iveagh in October 1953, a subscription arrangement was set up whereby each employee contributed 5 shillings to a fund. From this, a bound volume with the names of the three thousand employees was presented to the Iveaghs. The balance of the fund was set aside by the Board to go towards the education of sons or daughters of employees. Initially, this was £20 per year; it was later increased to £40, then £50, and later £60. It finished completely in July 1974, when the sum of £71.08 was awarded. Also on the occasion of the Golden Wedding, the Board made a presentation of a wireless system to Dr Steevens Hospital.[95]

THE BLUE BOOK

The 'Blue Book' came into its own during the depression of the 1940s and 1950s. It was basically a loan society, supported by the company, similar to the Credit Unions of a generation later. There were similar societies in operation in Dublin, one in Francis Street and another at Mount Brown.

To the ordinary worker, the Blue Book was a godsend. In the twentieth century, cash was king: all transactions were in cash, and family finances were determined by the amount that came in every week from the wage earner of the household. In many cases, the budgeting was done by the woman of the house, with cash being put aside in tin boxes, biscuit tins, envelopes and under the bed.

Budgeting had to be done for weekly household necessities,

with small amounts being put aside for capital purchases like furniture or bedding. Holidays had to be saved for, as did special occasions like family weddings, First Holy Communions and Confirmations. In many communities, the local shopkeeper acted as a credit facilitator for families that could be trusted to pay up on payday. The credit or 'tick' system abounded. Where it didn't, the moneylender preyed on people's need for cash for special occasions.

The pawn shop, or 'pop-shop', was also a thriving part of the Dublin social scene. Items were given in as security on a short-term loan, possibly a few days. There was an endless cycle of pawning items on a Monday after the weekend for cash until payday. The items were then redeemed on a Friday, just in time for the weekend, and returned on Monday. Bearing in mind the fact that Dubliners were mainly church-going, the most popular item pawned was the 'good suit', which was needed for church on Sunday but was not required again until the following Sunday. Therefore it made sense to pawn the suit – or, in the case of a large family, several suits – on a Monday, have the cash for food during the week, and then redeem the suit again on Friday or Saturday when the family had the cash to do so.

In the Brewery, the Blue Book was a cash loan society. Cash was requested for a specific purpose, mainly holidays or family occasions. The request was initially considered by the treasurer of the time, who, if the sum was not large, had the discretion to give it out. If a large sum was involved, the request went to a committee. Generally, the treasurer advised the committee, and the recipient promised to repay a certain amount every week from his pay packet. In many instances, the treasurer was also the timekeeper who handed out the pay packets and, as such, could hold out his hand for the repayment. In the case of a refusal to pay up, the offending debtor could be taken before the manager of the department, who would then persuade the debtor to agree for a set amount to be deducted from his wages.

There were several Blue Book societies throughout the brewery. The Cooperage one was begun in 1892; the Racking one dates from 1913. There was one in the Traffic Department and one in the Engineers Department called 'The Engineers Workmen's Thrift and Loan Fund Society'. The Brewhouse was a late entry to the system, being founded in 1938 with the following committee: R. S. Wix (president), E. A. McNair (vice-president), C. Doherty (chairman), R. Switzer (vice-chairman), J. Breen (secretary), and P. Corcoran (treasurer). The ordinary committee members were J. Myles, J. Curran, M. Breslin, M. Farrell, F. McNally and E. Maher.

The Blue Book rules included provisions for fines of one penny in the pound per week of arrears. There was also a levy of one shilling per member as a mortality benefit, payable to the next of kin, not to exceed £20.[96]

THE GUINNESS PERMANENT BUILDING SOCIETY

The GPBS, as it was known, was founded in 1901 for the purpose of advancing loans to employees for the purchase of houses. It wasn't until 1918, however, that workmen were elected to the committee. Figures for 1911 show that there were 125 members and that £2485 was advanced that year. The Society seems to have reached a peak in 1937, when it had 622 members and the total advanced was £375,000. The rules at the time stated that, to get a loan of £700 for a house, a member needed to have at least £87 on deposit.

Purchasing a house for £700 was a huge step at the time, when the rent on a three-roomed flat in the Iveagh Trust ranged from four shillings and ninepence to seven shillings and sixpence, and to rent a house in Iveagh Gardens cost between nineteen and twenty-four shillings.[97]

The Society flourished until 1978, when it had 1300 members and advanced £427,680 in fifty-five loans. Shortly afterwards, the Society closed, transferring all its business to the First National Building Society, later to become the First Active Building Society.

PAY-PACKET DEDUCTIONS

In the days of cash payment, there was a variety of reasons why cash was deducted from pay packets. These reasons were mainly associated with family responsibilities and were arranged through either the Registry Department or the Medical Department.

Some were related to a man's reluctance or refusal to meet family financial responsibilities, either through alcoholism, gambling or a family disagreement. In these cases, the man would be asked to sign away part of his pay packet. The packet would be issued in the normal way, with the full amount of cash. When it reached the Labour Office or Time Office, the packet would be put aside and not paid out to the man.

In due course, later in the day, the packet would be delivered to either the Registry Department or the Medical Department, where it would be opened and an appropriate amount paid out to the man's family. Finally, the packet would be resealed and eventually handed to the man.

THE 1959 BICENTENARY

The year 1959 marked the bicentenary of the founding of the Guinness Brewery at St James's Gate in Dublin by the first Arthur Guinness. In the years leading up to 1959, there were many indications that this would be the celebration to end all celebrations. In many respects, the occasion marked a culmination of sorts for the culture of Guinnesses.

In the lead-up to the Bicentenary, the Guinness family were cautiously quiet and self-effacing. Many newspapers sought to write up the 'Guinness story' from different angles. Some looked at the historical angle, others at the business-success story, the personalities, or the Guinness dynasty. Some wrote about the 'bad-luck syndrome' which was said to afflict the family. (In almost every generation of the Guinness family in the twentieth century, there were tragic sudden deaths. For instance, Oonagh Guinness, Lady Oranmore and Browne, lost her son Tara in a car crash in London in the 1950s.) In all cases, throughout the 1950s, when there were requests to write articles, newspaper reports and even books, there was a marked reluctance on the part of the family to agree, to the extent of discouraging such writings. A phrase used in connection with one particular draft was that it was 'cheap journalese'.

Eventually, a supplement, written by selected writers, including the talented and already published Lord Moyne under his family name, Bryan Guinness, was produced to tell the Guinness story. Also at this time, two approved researchers, Patrick Lynch and John Vaisey, were working on an academic history book entitled *Guinness's Brewery in the Irish Economy, 1759–1876,* which was eventually published in 1960. Above all, the period leading up to the Bicentenary was a heady time of 'jollification' for the company.

Around 1958, there was a recognition that the bad old days of the 1940s and 1950s were at an end. Nationally, the Irish people, under government leader Sean Lemass, were gaining in self-confidence. The economy was improving and smog-ridden Dublin was about to shed its belted overcoat for a brighter, cleaner image.

A feature of that year was the new magazine published by the staff of the Press Office at St James's Gate, called simply *'The Harp'*. The first edition featured, not surprisingly, an article on the O'Neill harp, as well as on the St James's Gate windmill. The magazine initiated a series on the brewing process and began this with a feature on the First Mash in the Brewhouse. Other features covered the general news at St James's Gate, giving much-needed publicity to the Brewery societies, the Drama Group, the Annual Entertainment, the Musical Society and the Orphans' Aid Society.

Later editions of the magazine in 1958 carried photographs

of newly appointed members of staff, covered the Fermentation Department and showed a photograph of the Guinness lady clerks, resplendent in their overalls, operating the latest trade technology, the Hollerith accounts machines. More importantly, the magazine featured general social news, births, marriages, deaths and obituaries. Indeed, the second edition contained the obituary of my own father, Paddy Corcoran, written by Matt Kirwan. In addition, there were articles of general interest and others of historical importance.

For the Bicentenary year, there was a return to old-style philanthropy by the members of the Guinness family. A visit was made to the old Guinness home at Beaumont, then the Beaumont Convalescence Home, by Lord and Lady Iveagh on 21 July 1959.

For the Guinness workers, the highlight of the year was the Fireworks Display, which formed part of the Sixty-fourth Annual Fanciers' Show in the Iveagh Grounds on Saturday 11 July. Although the Fanciers' Show could be visited on that day, once darkness fell, admission to the Fireworks Display was by ticket only. In a format reminiscent of the Queen Victoria Days in the Royal Dublin Society grounds in the years preceding the Great War, entry to the fireworks display was controlled so that 'staff' (management) had different tickets from 'non-staff' (manual workers). There were also two entrance gates to the grounds, one for 'staff' and one for 'non-staff'. Inside the grounds, however, there was little attempt to control who mingled with whom.

There was also a personal gift for each employee of a china dish, which could be used either as a butter dish or an ashtray, featuring a portrait of Arthur Guinness the First. In addition, the postal service issued a commemorative stamp, also bearing the image the first Arthur.

As part of the events to mark the Bicentenary, the Guinness family made a gift to the Guinness workers of the Bicentenary Centre. This was a highly prized centre, to be built in Watling Street, due north of the Rupert Guinness Hall, and containing a gymnasium, a squash court, meeting rooms and a swimming pool. The foundation stone was laid by Lord Iveagh in 1959 and the building was officially opened on 2 April 1962 by Lord Moyne.

The Guinness Swimming Pool was a jewel in the crown of the sports facilities available to Guinness employees. For many years, it was enjoyed fully by all employees. At the time, it was one of only a small number of pools in Dublin; those using it were the envy of other Dubliners. Many ploys were used by interlopers who were not Guinness employees to gain admittance for a swim. One was simply to say that they had forgotten their ticket. A quizzing by the security man as to which department they or their parent worked in naturally, followed. One man always used the same excuse, saying that he worked in 'The Broken Yard'!

The Bicentenary year concluded with a Service of Thanksgiving on 31 December 1959 at the family's beloved St Patrick's Cathedral, no doubt in the company of the spirits of the Guinness ancestors and the Guinness workers over the previous two hundred years. As many of the workers of the time were Catholic and attendance at a non-Catholic service was frowned upon by the then Roman Catholic Archbishop, Dr John Charles McQuaid, there was a separate Mass of Thanksgiving at St James's Church, beside the brewery in James's Street.

8

THE PERSONNEL STRUCTURE IN GUINNESS

Some have said that the Guinness Brewery in Dublin was run like the British Army, while others have compared it with the Colonial Service of Great Britain. In many ways, both comparisons are accurate.

Ireland was a colony of the British Empire – and a very close one at that. Before the Act of Union, in the very early days of the Guinness Brewery, Dublin was the playground of the British aristocracy. After the Act of Union took effect, there was a retreat among the aristocracy, and the role of Dublin in the Empire diminished. The native Irish, in the eyes of the British, changed from amusing people to 'natives'. The situation worsened from the mid-nineteenth century, when the effects of the Famine helped turn Dublin into a city of poverty and disease. The British attitude to 'natives', in whatever part of the Empire, was that they were expected to know their place: to be servile. In Britain, this was reinforced by the class system which, in turn, was a holdover from the Victorian era.

In Ireland, however, the 1916 Rising and the Civil War changed all that. Certainly the Guinness family adapted well to the Irish Free State and engaged confidently with the new Irish Civil Service on such matters as Excise Duties and the various trade regulations. Yet the management at St James's Gate, right up to the 1970s, remained, in some respects, in a time warp, with a style reminiscent of Raffles Hotel in Singapore in the 1930s. Structures were so rigid that up to seven different dining rooms, for workers of various grades, existed at James's Gate. Indeed, this phenomenon even extended to the Workmen's Dining Rooms, in that the foremen and supervisors dined separately from the ordinary workers. The Dublin workers certainly knew how to mimic their superiors.

Broadly, Guinness employees were divided into directors, brewers, chemists, engineers, No. 1 staff, No. 2 staff, lady clerks, technical assistants, supervisors, foremen, coopers, tradesmen, labourers, lads and boys. The Guinness doctors fitted in somewhere between the brewers and the chemists.

At the top four levels of the structure, there was a culture of employing upper-class British graduates from Oxford or Cambridge University. These were all Protestant Conservatives connected either to the Guinness family or to the British royal family – either connection being of the same value as the other. On a regular basis, a 'brewer' would arrive at St James's Gate, complete with tweed jacket and posh accent, and driving a car with the emblem 'Austin of England'.

In Guinness terms, a 'brewer' was a Very Important Person, a senior manager – and due homage had to be paid to him at all times. Possibly because many brewers had science degrees, there was intense rivalry between the brewers and the chemists. This goes back to the mid-nineteenth century, when the Guinness family recruited the first chemist. The chemists had two very important functions. The first was to perfect the brewing process by dealing with any problems in the brewing process and proposing solutions. Brewing is, after all, a biochemical process involving barley, malt, hops, yeast, water and, most importantly, clean plant and processes. The second duty of the chemists was research and development.

The bulk of Guinness workers were employed as labourers. Brewing, up to the 1970s, was a labour-intensive business. Big, strong men were required at all stages of the process, including carrying large sacks of barley and malt. Hops came in sacks about twelve feet high; dexterity as well as strength was needed to manoeuvre them. While the mashing process was mechanical, the 'spent' grains needed to be shovelled out manually while they were still hot. This required a team of semi-naked men wearing canvas trousers and wooden clogs to climb into the kieve – a large circular vessel into which the mash of grain and hot water is poured at the start of the brewing process – and work in conditions of high humidity to 'turn round' the vessel for the next mash as quickly as possible. Similar conditions existed in the coppers from which the 'spent' hops had to be removed.

After the fermentation process had occurred, the surplus yeast needed to be removed and processed to remove surplus beer from it – because excise duty had been paid on the full volume. Again, the fermentation vessel had to be cleaned and sterilised in time for the next batch. This required groups of men, up to the 1980s, to enter the vessel – first ensuring that all carbon dioxide gas had been removed. Other vessels further down the process stream also required a major input of manual labour.

The despatch end of the operation was equally labour-intensive. Wooden casks, and later metal casks, needed to be cleaned and filled. These casks then had to be rolled into lofts and placed on drays, cars and railway wagons for despatch all over Ireland. On the export side, the casks were transferred to barges for a short journey down the River Liffey to the waiting cross-Channel steamers, into which they were lifted and stowed for their journey to the British and foreign trade.

Small wonder, then, that the labour force in the Guinness brewery often exceeded five thousand men. In addition, there were many people working in all the back-up services, including the general stores, the cleaners, the huge engineering workshop, and in security and catering.

Looking after all of these was the Medical Department, which not only cared for the workers but also delivered first-class primary care to their families. Wages were paid by the Accountants' Department in a cash office designed in Victorian times. Cash receipts on the other side were managed by the Trade Department, which was staffed mainly by lady clerks who looked after the invoicing of the customers and receipt of the monies.

Throughout the organisation were the ubiquitous messengers. This was the starting point in the careers of many of Guinness workers. Much research has been done on the messenger system, which recruited boys aged thirteen years and eleven months.[98] There was a competitive examination each year, which was eagerly awaited by many working-class Dublin families. The target candidates were the sons of Guinness workers, as well as others whose families saw the opportunity to transfer the youngsters from school to a job which would ultimately be well paid. Recruited messengers were given a uniform – including shirts with heavily starched, detachable collars, and shoes – which was regularly replaced. Those aged fourteen to eighteen were given a superb free four-course lunch in the Boys' Dining Room. For healthy, hungry young men, this lunch was a delicious break from work: the workers sat on long benches and reached into the centre of the table for the floury potatoes. They were eligible to join the Guinness Athletic Union and could play the sport of their choice in the Iveagh Grounds in Crumlin.

This system benefited both the company and the boys. Because the examination was a competitive one, those who applied were the better ones in the local Christian Brothers' schools – the students who, in another age, would have been university material.

With the company's encouragement, these boys attended technical school after they had commenced work. The company paid the fees and monitored their attendance and the assessment results. Prizes were awarded for good results, and extra summer leave was granted for perfect attendance. Many gained Leaving Certificates and went on to attend university in the evening, graduating in subjects such as business, commerce and accountancy. Others stayed with the technical school and went on to achieve a Bachelor of Science degrees with London University. Consequently, Guinness had well-educated young men entering the workforce.

Within the company, there were other opportunities for these young men aged between eighteen and twenty-one. In a system reminiscent of the army system of non-commissioned officers, these lads were invited to go for another competitive examination, for the No. 2 staff. Many succeeded and became the backbone of the management structure of the company.

For the first half of the twentieth century, as we have seen, entry to the No. 1 staff was restricted to young men with 'connections'. What was important was that they were of 'officer' material. To the workers, many of these 'mini-brewers' had strange accents and a superior attitude.

This situation seemed to give some comfort to the Guinness senior management. They felt that the company was in the hands of people to whom they could relate. One commentator of the day who was raised in the Protestant tradition in Dublin spoke of being sent away to boarding school in England for a number of reasons. One was to acquire the 'right' accent and the other was to learn how to 'rule the Empire'.[99]

And rule the Guinness empire was what they did. In many cases, however, there were problems with the labourers – these 'rough fellows', as they were once described by a typical No. 1 staff manager. But the recruitment of the No. 2 staff from amongst the messengers and labourers addressed this. They acted as buffers in dealing with process orders. At the same time, however, there was a large element of snobbery, which manifested itself in gossip and barbed comments over lunch: unfortunately for some, the No. 1, No. 2, and Ladies' Staffs all dined in the same dining room.

There were some difficulties surrounding where exactly one sat in the dining room. Officially, there was no set seating arrangements. Unofficially, of course, there were strict unwritten protocols about who sat where. Certain individuals believed they had a set place at a set table in the company of set people. This arrangement was fine until a stranger arrived in the dining room seeking a seat. He (or she) could decide to sit at a particular table where there was a vacant seat, asking the strange question: 'Is there someone sitting here?' If there was no reply from the others at the table, or a frosty look, then he took his life – and his digestion – in his hands if he sat there. Sometimes the person who believed it was *his* seat would arrive later and there was an even frostier exchange of words. One displaced gentleman solved this particular problem to his satisfaction by licking his thumb and then putting it into the intruder's soup! There was also a gamble involved in *not* sitting down. In this case, one stood, looking lost and uneasy, until the Head Waiter, resplendent in dinner jacket and bow tie, placed you at a table – where, once again, you were not made welcome.

But from the middle of the 1950s, several changes took place. A more enlightened company management began to see the advantage of local management comprised of local talent. The No. 2 staff recruitment ceased; it was replaced by a group, drawn from messengers and laboratory attendants, called technical assistants. These eager young men – and, in latter years, young women as well – had capabilities in both the management and technical fields, .

The technical assistants had the ability to rule the newly dawned Guinness Dublin structure. They were acceptable to management and, in particular, were acceptable to the workforce because they were from their own culture. Gradually, in the 1960s, 1970s and 1980s, the Protestant domination of the Guinness management became irrelevant and working-class Catholics, many of whom had fathers and uncles working as labourers, took over the management roles in a more enlightened Guinness Brewery. Even entry to the revered No. 1 Staff became more achievable through qualifications and interview.

There was, however, a stopgap measure. Again, using the principle that local knowledge is best, the company had always promoted men who showed most potential into foremen. The system was simple. The objective was to get the job done efficiently and effectively. Before the advent of trade unions, the men who showed most potential got the chance. They were observed in their roles as workers and in terms of their ability to get on with their fellow workers. Teamwork was a key quality. In addition, literacy was important – the ability to read and understand instructions, to write reports, to calculate hours worked and overtime which needed to be paid. These men were very similar to the No. 2 staff in many ways, except that they were closer to the work ethic and knew their men well.

Within the workforce, the foremen generally built up respect for their position. Generally, they were very astute and it was extremely difficult to fool them. If you look back on their family history, you will find that many were from Guinness families and had a heritage of serving the company. For the most part, they would have entered the company with very high marks in the boy's examination at age fourteen. Snobbery also existed at the foreman level, however. There is a story told of a department where the senior foreman wore a white coat on the job while his juniors wore buff coats. When the senior foreman went to lunch, the most senior of his juniors would take off his buff coat and wear the white coat for the duration of the senior man's lunchtime.

In the 1950s, the Board of Guinness was in the control of a personnel director called Sir Charles Harvey, referred to as 'C.O.H.' He began restructuring the workforce to take account of world trends in industrial relations and the management of workers. Thus, from the group of foremen, there emerged a new title – Supervisor – which was established in 1955.[100] The more powerful and astute foremen were promoted to Supervisor. The post was paid monthly and the Supervisors were almost all from Brewery families. They quickly formed an alliance with each other and became a powerful influence in local management. Many had sons who had also entered the workforce, and these young men were carefully watched and groomed by the supervisory group.

The Ladies' Staff more or less mirrored the No. 1 staff, but the changes there happened much earlier. The first recorded employment of ladies was on 9 October 1900, as an experiment. The salary given was £1 per week, with a Miss Hunter as superintendent at £1 10 shillings per week. There is a record of a competitive examination for temporary female clerks on 25 February

1905. The record, in naming the successful candidates, also refers to them as being 'relatives of employees'.[101]

By the 1940s, there was regular recruitment of lady clerks from various secretarial colleges in Dublin – many of them run by nuns – such as Loreto College, Crumlin, which was within the residential area of many Guinness workers, and Dominican College in Eccles Street. Girls would apply to these colleges after completing the Leaving Certificate, to be trained in shorthand and typing. For the purpose of selection, there was close co-operation between the Guinness Lady Superintendent and the nuns who managed these colleges.

Once inside the Guinness gates, the girls found a strict regime of discipline, with styles reminiscent of Victorian days, where a supervisor of each office would sit at a high desk over-seeing the work. Junior girls were expected to dine in the staff dining room at the noon lunch, which was for girls only. Only the more senior ladies could attend the later lunch sittings and mingle with the men. Nonetheless, there was some mingling between the sexes through the sports clubs and the Guinness Choir and Drama Group. There was also the regular 'tea dances' held in one of the Guinness houses, 98 James's Street (encouraged by Sir Charles), for which one had to receive an invitation.

While at work in the offices, girls were expected to wear shapeless overalls in dark blue, presumably to avoid the dangers of tempting the men during office hours. For the most part, the girls did as they were instructed, although occasionally a rebel would appear wearing a pink overall or, indeed, her normal clothes. It remained so until the late 1960s and early 1970s, when overalls were shed in favour of miniskirts after the sexual revolution of California and Carnaby Street finally reached St James's Gate.

The Lady Superintendents, it must be said, had a close interest in all the ladies under their remit. At times, it may have been a controlling interest, like the case of a young lady who had a biro mark placed on her knee to indicate the point to which her overall should reach. At other times, it was a kindly interest. If, at certain times of the month, a young lady felt unwell or emotional, she was sent to the Lady Superintendent by her supervisor. If all that was required was a sympathetic hearing, a cup of tea and a 'lie down', there was a couch in the Lady Superintendent's office for that purpose. For the young ladies who wished to announce their engagement to their work colleagues, there was a strict protocol. Before the engagement ring could be shown to her colleagues, she had to see the Lady Superintendent and announce her engagement to her. The ring could then be produced and admired by the Lady Superintendent, followed by a background check on the intended spouse. Where relevant, a suitable approval reckoning was given. Where the intended spouse was a company employee, there was a special approval process, in which his work record, his family record and his future prospects in the company were discussed. After all that, the lady could return to her workplace, formally announce her engagement and show the ring to her friends and colleagues.

Knowing this procedure was an advantage for young male suitors. In one case, advance arrangements were made to have a large bouquet of flowers delivered to the young lady's workplace. Later on the day of the announcement, this information was relayed to the Lady Superintendent, who took it on herself to visit the workplace and pronounce herself delighted with the flowers, the young man and the gesture.

Within the Guinness Brewery, there were two other groups of female workers. The waitresses in the Catering (or Refreshment) Department served food in the various dining rooms, but chiefly in the two main areas: the staff dining room at St James's Gate, where men and women management staff dined at tables seating either four or six people, complete with linen table cloths and silver cutlery, and the workers' dining room at Belview, which had long dining tables seating about twenty and which did not have tablecloths. Eventually, with the shift to contract catering, these women were offered severance packages or transfers to other Guinness departments, where some, after retraining, excelled in such physical work as forklift driving.

Another group of female workers were the office cleaners. These women were recruited from amongst the Guinness widows who were offered employment to supplement their widow's pensions. This writer's maternal grandmother commenced such work in April 1916, an auspicious date in Irish history.

The 'widows' were not always widows. With increased pension rights and support from their families, many widows chose not to accept such work. The work was then offered out to other female relatives of Guinness workers. In some cases, the connection was a tenuous one. Indeed, some of the women were not always capable of the physical work demanded of them. Some had minor physical handicaps, and others may have had what would now be called special needs, but they were always taken on in a genuine spirit of Guinness generosity. Indeed, I remember a conversation with one woman who told the story of her brother who had died 'without regaining conscience'. There was always close rapport between such women and the various messenger boys in the offices and the laboratories. The eventual drive to reduce costs led to the disbandment of this system and the employment of contract cleaners.

So how have the personnel structures in Guinness changed since the business was founded in 1759? To begin with, the company was, until 1886, a family firm. As such, employment was the personal choice of the various family members. If the Guinness family knew a man, there was a good chance he would be taken on. Nonetheless, many mistakes were made, and numerous employees, including members of the Guinness family, were asked to leave. Many were simply sacked for incompetence or misbehaviour. Structures were put in place for physical and medical attributes. (As the duties of a labourer involved heavy physical work, such as moving huge sacks of hops or digging grain, physical attributes like weight, height and chest measurement were specified for those being employed. It was even specified that those employed should have good teeth!)

On the management side, the company always played safe and recruited in a conservative way. This caused much angst on the part of the increasingly well-educated local, Catholic – and thus nationalist – workforce, who saw a bias in favour of Protestants. Indeed, this was so, but was probably due to excessive caution on the part of management. With the advent of trade unionism in the mid-twentieth century, this bias was eventually broken down, thus allowing free access through the ranks for all, based on work competence.

This arrangement was to soon be overtaken by other events, however. Increased competition and profit margins, reduced staff numbers brought about by the inevitable move to mechanisation, and responsibility to shareholders all came into play in the latter part of the twentieth century.

With increased mechanisation came many welcome changes. A lot of the relatively unskilled manual work was eliminated. Older workers were given the opportunity to accept voluntary retirement with relatively good pensions.

A skills audit showed that different technical skills were required. These skills were dormant in many of the younger people in the workforce, both male and female, and they were quickly encouraged to demonstrate them.

Thus the old social barriers were removed. Quality programmes such as ISO 9002, an international standard of work procedures and processes, were introduced. The resultant workforce profile was one where skills were recognised for their worth, regardless of people's background or gender. But then, in line with most companies worldwide, there was an inevitable refocusing on results and the bottom line. The entire workforce, in a short period, became results-focused, but also somewhat impersonal. Guinness Dublin became part of Guinness Ireland and then part of the huge multi-national company the Diageo Corporation. The personal care and interest by the Guinness family, so generously shown in other times, had been replaced by a more modern style of recruitment and management.

9

INDUSTRIAL RELATIONS IN GUINNESSES

This chapter is not a definitive or academic account of Guinness industrial relations but rather an account of the interactions that took place between Guinness management and workers over a fifty-year period. During the early part of the twentieth century, there was much unrest amongst the workers in Dublin in general. The various forms of nationalism blurred into socialism and the workers movement, and there was political unrest. Guinness workers remained faithful to their employer – with some exceptions. As we have seen, the period of the 1916 Rising caused serious rifts in the employer-worker relationship when those who absented themselves from work without permission were eventually sacked.

In 1924, the employers of Dublin formed the Dublin Employers' Emergency Committee to 'support the rights of employers to conduct business . . . and to ensure reasonable control over their staffs'. Letters were exchanged between the Guinness company and other employers, including the Jacobs biscuit factory in Dublin. There was not much reaction to this from the Guinness workers, who seemed to be content with their lot.[102]

In the previous year, while there was serious unemployment in Dublin, some of those without jobs noted that Guinness workers were not only enjoying the benefits of their employment but doing 'nixers' in the evening. This resulted in a strong letter being sent to the company from the Council of the Unemployed.

Some decades later, a significant date in the company's history was May 1946, when the Association of Brewery Employees – a house association – was formed. Despite claims that the association did not represent the majority, it became formally established, with the following officers: Michael Kiersey (chairman), Tom Spollen (vice-chairman), Peter Nevin (honorary secretary), Jack Prior (assistant honorary secretary) and William Billings (honorary treasurer).[103]

The association had a yearly subscription of two shillings; in November 1946 it acquired an office at 14 Thomas Street. An analysis undertaken at the time showed that the membership consisted of 34.6 percent graded men, 54.6 percent ungraded men and 16.9 percent lads and boys. Dealings were conducted mainly with the Second Brewer, Mr Buttenshaw. Some small advances were granted, such as Grades 1 and 1A men to have attendance and payment recorded separately from others. Further advances were then sought, the most significant being, in February 1948, a claim to the Labour Court for the right to negotiate on behalf of the workers. The Labour Court hearing began on 27 February 1948, but the issue was unresolved.

In the company submission, Sir Charles Harvey stated that it would be more satisfactory for the workers to join a regular trade union. Later, he sent a message to all the men saying that he was not prepared to accept the house association as it was then constituted and that he proposed the setting up of a Works Committee as then existed at Park Royal, the Guinness brewery in London.

A general meeting was called by the committee to take place in the Mansion House in Dublin on Sunday 29 May 1949. Preceding the meeting were proposals from both the Irish Transport and General Workers' Union and Jim Larkin's Workers' Union of Ireland. These were reported in the *Irish Press* of 27 May. The *Daily Mail* of the same date reported that two thousand Guinness workers were about to join a trade union.

Reports subsequent to the meeting tell different stories.[104] The *Irish Press* stated that a thousand men were present and that the meeting broke up in disorder. Reports stated that one delegate shouted 'Communists!' at the committee and was asked to withdraw the remark. The delegate refused to withdraw the remark, tore up his membership card and left the meeting in protest. On the other hand, there is a letter to the editor on 31 May 1949 from Michael Kiersey stating that there was no disorder at the meeting. The eventual outcome was a majority decision to transfer membership to the Workers' Union of Ireland. Arrangements were made for Jim Larkin to address a reconvened meeting on 9 June 1949.

Back at the Brewery, there was concern amongst those opposed to union membership, and a new Guinness Employees' Association was formed by J. Byrne, T. Connors, P. Kinane, K. Raynor and T. Creighton. This situation continued until September 1951, when the General Secretary of the Workers' Union of Ireland satisfied the Guinness Board that the union represented the majority of the non-craft workers.[105]

THE ST JAMES'S GATE SENIOR FOREMEN'S ASSOCIATION

This association could be seen as a microcosm of the culture among Guinness workers in the 1950s. Resulting from a perceived isolation of Guinness workers following the establishment of the Workers' Union of Ireland, there emerged a need for the 'senior foremen' to organise themselves into some formal structure. The senior foremen, positioned between the workers and management, saw themselves as a form of management: bearing in mind the work they did, this was indeed true.

They were the funnel through which the management staff issued instructions, thus relieving management of the need to get involved directly with the workers. The senior foremen who passed on management's instructions saw themselves as power brokers when, it might be argued, that they were simply the messengers of management. This, indeed was how the workers saw their foremen, and they treated the senior foremen accordingly. The resulting tensions had a number of effects. Firstly, the senior foremen, some of whom became Supervisors at a later date, became strong and fair in their dealings with both sides. Secondly, they gained universal respect. Nonetheless, their position was clearly a company one, as they always had the interests of the company at heart. Both the brewing foremen and the engineering foremen were similar people, despite their rivalries. Nonetheless, the time had come, in 1953, for the foremen to become organised. The minutes recorded that:

> The inaugural meeting was held in the Visitors' Waiting Room on Wednesday 4 March 1953. Present were Messrs Farnan, Ivers, P. O'Brien, Greene, Doggett, O'Toole, Brennan, Cowman, Carrick, D. O'Brien, Smiley and O'Connell. Mr P. Parker was absent on a jury.[106]

Even the last sentence is important. To serve on a jury meant, firstly, that the man was a householder, and secondly, that the valuation of his house property was above a certain level. The rules of the association stated in the first article:

> That this group shall be called 'The St James's Gate Brewery Senior Foremen's Association'. The objects of the association shall be at all times to foster the interests of the Brewery and to bring closer and more friendly cooperation between the members and the Board of Directors.[107]

The rules went on to state that membership was by application and was confined to Supervisors 1 and 2 Grade, trades group, and Supervisors, 1A, 1B and 1 Grade, non-trades group. An annual subscription was agreed upon, and there were complex rules about presentations to members on retirement. The committee was also empowered to terminate the membership of any member for 'non-payment of subscriptions . . . without just cause, and for conduct which may bring the association into disrepute.' The final rule of the Association was that its aim was to render all possible help to dependants of deceased members. In effect, this meant a cash gratuity to the widow on the death of a member.

In the minutes of some of the early meetings, there is a theme of seeking a specific slot in the Brewery hierarchy. A status statement was required; this was evident in a report to one meeting in which a member of the association took issue with a member of staff regarding the way in which a letter was addressed to him. This resulted in an apology from the member of staff. At another meeting, a member had a conversation with the Lady Superintendent in which she agreed 'to take steps to see that the Ladies' Staff would in future show proper respect to the members of our group'.

A major event in the Association's calendar was the Annual Dinner, to which those who had retired in the previous twelve months were invited and at which they were presented with an umbrella and a 'wallet of notes'. The umbrellas and wallets were to be purchased from a specialist umbrella shop called Smyth's. Invitations were sent to Sir Charles Harvey and Michael Morrissey, Labour Manager.

The venue for the dinner was agreed in the early years as the Swiss Chalet, a popular Dublin restaurant of the time, and two committee members were designated to visit said premises to make the necessary arrangements some weeks in advance. Artistes were engaged for the entertainment and, at the meeting in September 1953, it was agreed to engage two singers, two comedians and a pianist – at a fee of one guinea each.[108]

The toasts at the dinner were carefully planned and orchestrated. In 1954, the Chairman, Mr Farnan, was to propose the first toast to 'Ireland', the next toast was proposed by Mr Connell to 'the Brewery', Mr Parker would propose 'the Guests' and Mr Greene would propose 'the Artistes'.

In later years, the annual dinner was moved to the Refreshment Department, and the list of invitees included the whole Board of Directors and the labour manager. In one year, the finances of the association were tight; the committee, determined to invite everyone as usual, had an informal whip-around amongst themselves, each man contributing £1. While everyone always had a good time, there were instances of overconsumption of the good product by the odd miscreant. Once or twice an offender was observed on the following day still under the influence of alcohol. In every case, the committee saw fit to summon the offenders to a special meeting, where they were accused of bringing the association 'into disrepute' and a formal apology was sought – and always given.

In relation to dining, it is interesting to note that the senior foremen were given their own dining area in the general 'workmen's rooms' in Belview. This was an annexe of the main dining room, with a number of smaller tables, which was shut off from the general workers. Having achieved this privilege, the senior foremen sought to restrict this arrangement to the 'senior' foremen. Hence, when a 'junior' foreman was seen using the room, this fact was mentioned at the next committee meeting and a senior member of the committee was deputed to speak to him and to ask him to desist. It should also be noted that, within two years, the said junior foreman became a senior foreman and, in addition to being then eligible for the privileged dining room, became a useful member of the committee. Some time later, when the dining room was an accepted privilege, the senior foremen pushed their luck a little too far and asked for a separate entrance to their room directly from the street. The company refused.

Sir Charles Harvey included the senior foremen in his initiatives relating to training and new methods of work. Talks were given at regular intervals in the Rupert Guinness Hall for management, and the senior foremen were pleased to be invited to attend. They were also included in training courses being run by the College of Commerce in Rathmines and in the Brewery on various issues, including work study. At the time, the term 'work study' was misunderstood: there was a perception that work-study officers, with their clipboards and stopwatches, represented a sneaky attempt to make people work harder, and this misunderstanding created a great deal of suspicion.

Concern for the families of members is evident for this writer, when one reads the minutes of the meeting of 2 April 1958:

> Payment of full benefit to the widow of the late Mr P. Corcoran was agreed to; the committee noted with satisfaction the action of the Board in making possible an appointment to the Technical Assistant Staff for the son of our late member.

The minutes of the Association through the late 1950s and into the early 1960s eventually took on the obvious concerns regarding grading of posts and negotiations with the Board. Interspersed with this were occasional letters of congratulation to various members and Board members, including a telegram to Lord Iveagh on the occasion of his birthday. On a compassionate note, in April 1961 there were good wishes sent to a member who was ill, wishing him a speedy recovery, and there was an agreement to send him a gift of cigarettes to the value of £1.

Through the 1960s, there was the inevitable poaching of members by the Workers' Union of Ireland, the formation of new committees, and the eventual transfer of most senior foremen to the Workers' Union of Ireland, thus signalling the end of the non-unionised Senior Foremen's Association.

10

Passing on the Caring

Guinness's generosity began with the compassionate nature of the Guinness family, which has been passed through the ranks of the family right up to the present day.

After Arthur Guinness began his business in 1759 at St James's Gate and took up residence at No. 1 Thomas Street, he is reputed to have treated his employees well. No doubt, being an astute businessman, he treated them fairly and in return expected loyalty, quality workmanship and hard work. He valued his reputation not only as a good employer but also as a social mover, as witness his marriage to Olivia Whitmore, cousin of Henry Grattan.

The second Arthur Guinness became a director and later governor of the Bank of Ireland and was a supporter of Daniel O'Connell and Catholic Emancipation. With the coming of the Victorian era, the family readily accepted the idea that their riches were a gift from God and, as such, were to be shared with the community. Benjamin Lee Guinness became Lord Mayor of Dublin and later Conservative MP for Dublin city. In 1865, he paid for the renovation of St Patrick's Cathedral from his personal finances.

Perhaps the most famous member of the Guinness family was Edward Cecil, later the First Earl of Iveagh, who set up the Guinness Trust, later the Iveagh Trust, in Dublin. His brother, Arthur Edward, devoted much time and money to the Dublin Artisans' Dwelling Company, of which he was chairman. He is also reputed to have purchased St Stephen's Green for the people of Dublin.

Over the centuries, Guinness workers were well paid in relation to the general working-class Dubliner. In addition, they had medical care, clothing allowances, food and fuel at reduced prices. Most importantly, they had pensions when most people had none.

The phrase 'from womb to tomb' encapsulated the Guinness worker culture. Small wonder, then, that many of the Guinness workers and their families took on the example of their employer and became charitable and compassionate people. The role of the Medical Department has already been outlined in the dispensing not just of medicine but of primary care where it was most needed – among the poor and underprivileged of Dublin. There are many examples of the generosity of the Guinness General Purposes Subcommittee, which met regularly to disburse charitable donations.

In 1897, the committee agreed to pay for an artificial arm for a man injured in an accident, paid gratuities to some workers to emigrate to Australia, and gave a donation to the City of Dublin Working Man's Club to pay for excursions for children. There is a record of a donation of £500 towards the distress fund being organised by the Lord Lieutenant. The committee donated 100 guineas to the Licensed Vintners Asylum and, at the same meeting, agreed to a sum to be given to a Norwegian sailor who had an accident at the North Wall with a ship's rope – described as being 'not the company's fault' – while loading Guinness casks.[109]

Donations were made to the Ringsend Technical School and Dolphins Barn School, as some of their pupils were from Guinness workers' families. A donation was also made through Findlaters for the Thornhill Colliery disaster fund, and a sum was paid out towards Harold's Cross People's Park.

In 1897, a donation of £3000 was made to the Queen's Jubilee Fund. After 1900, donations were made to the Royal Irish Association for promoting the training and employment of women, to the Mater Convalescent Hospital in Drumcondra and to the St James's Catholic Association. A contribution of £50 was made to the widows of the crew of the steamship *Marlay,* which foundered while bringing coal to Tedcastles.

There was agreement in 1908 to supply coal to the Guinness co-op store at sixpence per ton below the market price and for it to be delivered to Brewery employees. Membership of the Brewery co-op cost one shilling per annum – good value when you consider the savings in purchases.

Other initiatives included the Burial Allowance and the use of plots at Chapelizod for employees to grow vegetables. Most importantly, in 1915, the St James's Gate Health Insurance Society was established; this was a model for and forerunner of the Irish State National Health Scheme. Indeed, when the state scheme was being set up, the Brewery loaned Michael Morrissey, secretary of the Brewery society, to the Irish Civil Service to facilitate the set-up. There were also, as we have seen the various 'Blue Books' – the departmental loan societies.

Many charitable contributions were made on a discreet and confidential basis from the company to Dublin and local charities. Bearing in mind the religious affiliations of the staff and workforce, the contributions were divided between Catholic and Protestant charities. These contributions mainly took the form of food and clothing vouchers, which were delivered by hand by a small number of Guinness ladies to named charities, clergy and sisters.

All in all, the generosity of the Guinness family, the Guinness Board and Guinness management was a constant part of the culture at St James's Gate for more than two hundred years. So naturally, the workers took on this culture themselves. They saw how the Medical Department worked, how the Social Worker interacted with their families and dependants and how the company worked in conjunction with the local community. They were aware of how discretionary sick pay was given in deserving circumstances. They saw widows and orphans of past Guinness workers cared for, given food and clothing, and given discretionary pensions. In many cases, widows were given jobs as office cleaners.

Sometimes, workers, either through illness or accident, were unable to work any more. These were allowed to stay in the workforce if they wished. They were given 'light work', which sometimes amounted to walking around with a brush all day and chatting with those they met. These bore the nicknames 'the Walking Wounded' or 'the Lourdes Gangs'.

Also, at one time in the 1960s, the office cleaners consisted of some women with minor physical disabilities who were well able to do the duties required of them. There were also some with strange attitudes – like the woman who waited until the workers on the early shift had finished their breakfast in the mess room, and then 'took away' the remaining bread, butter, rashers and eggs. This was, in some ways, a good move, because the Catering Department always sent in a fresh supply for the next shift, regardless of what was left over.

In safer times, the Guinness worker was paid weekly in cash. This included shift allowances and overtime – all of which would have been detailed separately on the payslip. There are stories of unscrupulous men who only informed their wives of the basic payment, thus having the allowances and the overtime entirely for themselves. A story is told of the wife of a driver who inadvertently saw the total sum in the package. On accusing her husband of deception, she was told: 'But I have to pay my helper out of that!'

Having ready cash on payday meant many collections. In particular, on payday there were the familiar figures of the Little Sisters of the Poor who stood outside the Guinness Back Gate as the workers went out to lunch. Hail, rain or snow, these little ladies (they were always tiny) held out their collection boxes for the shillings and pence from the burly hands of the big Guinness workmen. While some of the proceeds of the collection probably went for the nuns' upkeep, they mainly redistributed the money to the poor from their convent in Kilmainham.

Eventually, due to dwindling numbers amongst the nuns and

the changeover from payment by cash to payment by bank transfer, the collections ceased. There was, however, an effort by a timekeeper called Paddy Stout to keep the collection going.

For a period of time in the 1950s and 1960s, the company decided, by way of a profit-sharing scheme, to award each employee an announced percentage of his or her annual pay. When payment was made in cash on Bonus Day, there was a huge amount of money in everyone's pockets. Collections were particularly successful on occasions like this. One collection stands out. The payment of the bonus was made to those permanently on the company books from April to the end of the year. Particularly amongst the boys, however, there were many taken on in their first year after April who were thus not entitled to a bonus for that year. There was always a whip-around amongst their colleagues to ensure that, although they might not get the same amount as everyone else, they did at least get something.

A particular charity, probably unofficial, was run amongst the Brewing Department. This was the 'Uncle Paddy' collection for children in hospital, conducted by Dan Condren of the Fermentation Department. In later years, a formal charity called 'Friends of St Raphael's' – a hospital for children with special needs – was set up in the company. This group organised special collections and ran concerts to raise funds for the treatment of these children.

There was a strange phenomenon within the Guinness Film Society. While the object of the Society was to import and show films of cultural significance, there was an annual Orphans' Party run by the Society's committee. The Rupert Guinness Hall was booked for a date close to Christmas, gifts and food were purchased and prepared, orphanages around Ireland were contacted, and transport was arranged to St James's Gate. Then, on the day itself, a group of volunteers would entertain these orphans and feed them sweets, jelly and ice cream. Then a rotund Santa Claus would appear and hand out gifts to the children. This was the highlight of the year, not just for the orphans but also for the volunteers. Eventually the scheme was abandoned because of falling numbers living in orphanages.

A very significant act of generosity by Guinness workers was the foundation, in 1958, of the Guinness Workers' Employment Fund, which is still active today. The idea for this came about as Guinness dockers, in 1957, were working at Custom House Quay in Dublin loading wooden casks into the Guinness ships for transportation to England. Further down the quay was the B&I ship, which sailed daily for Liverpool. This ship carried thousands of men every week to England looking for work: although there was still a recession in Ireland, work was available in England on building sites and on the start of an improved network of roads, which were to become the British motorways.

The Guinness dockers saw whole families walk down to the ship each day and return without the father of the family, who had sailed on the ship. They were also aware that, in the new suburbs of Dublin, around Walkinstown, there were families who had taken out a mortgage to start a new life and then, being unable to make the mortgage payments, had simply closed the door of the house, left the key in the door and departed to England with tears in their eyes.

The Workers' Union of Ireland had been established eight years previously; these scenes were described to a union meeting in the Mansion House. As a direct result, there was a resolution to start a fund to create employment in Ireland from the pay packets of Guinness workers. The initial concept was 'bob-a-job': each worker promised to contribute a shilling (a bob) a week to a fund to create employment. The money raised was used to give loans to people who wanted to start their own business. This money, when repaid, would be loaned out to other individuals for the same purpose.

When the concept of sponsored events, such as charity walks, became common, the workforce of Guinness was a rich source of income for the charities. With a complement of over three thousand people, and groups of several hundred in each department, those seeking sponsorship were well received and supported by their work colleagues.

In this respect, the boundaries of culture and religion were well breached. In matters of charity collections, whether for a Protestant or Catholic cause, the support was always the same. In latter years, the collections were for secular common causes, for the homeless, for the hospice movement, for the local children's hospital, even for the railway-preservation society of Ireland.

One incident springs to mind. Following a Brewery Council Safety quiz, I was on the runner-up team, which received a prize of £100 to be shared among the four of us. As the drinks on the night in question were sponsored, there was no need to fund a drinking spree, so it was suggested that I take the money in hand and give it to charity on behalf of the group. So, the next day, with £100 tucked into my pocket, I was on my way into work at 1.45 PM for the 2 o'clock shift when I remembered the 'Alone' Foundation, which had sponsored housing in Kilmainham for the elderly. I stopped at their office, handed over the cash and got a receipt. As time was short, the lady on duty, who had wanted to give me a tour of the complex, gave me, instead, a brochure of the charity and its work. In due course, I arrived at work, pinned the receipt to the noticeboard and left the brochure on the table.

The same day, one of my colleagues was on a training course at which the tutor offered a prize of £20 to the person who prepared and gave the best presentation on any subject the next day. My colleague studied the brochure (which had been left on the table in the mess room) and went on to win the £20, which was again handed to me to donate to 'Alone'. So, from one evening's safety quiz, the charity benefited to the tune of £120!

Another example of support was the Hospice Coffee Morning. Each year, a date is set in September, and there are coffee mornings all over Ireland. This meant, of course, that there were coffee mornings all over Guinness. So, for the coffee drinker who valued his or her reputation, it was important to attend as many as possible – without drinking too much coffee – and contributing to each one.

It must also be said that many Guinness worker, having been

shown charitable example by the company and having been exposed to many charity collections in the workplace, went on to be charitable people in their private and community lives. There are many examples of Guinness workers participating in and running charities and community initiatives such as loan societies (Mount Brown and Francis Street), being involved in St Vincent de Paul conferences in the city, and actively participating in their parishes. Guinness people were also involved in the Dublin Diocesan Pilgrimage to Lourdes, and there is a report in *The Harp* of two such men, Harry Bruce and Jim Corcoran, receiving Lourdes Confraternity medals in 1958.[110]

THE SOCIAL SCENE

It was recognised as far back as the first decade of the twentieth century, particularly by John Lumsden, that the workers in Guinness constituted, with their families, a community in itself. Having initially looked after the primary care of this community, Lumsden went on to involve the women of the Guinness community in classes on nutrition and domestic duties. He then moved on to arrange concerts for the women, and this initiative quickly developed into general concerts for all. In addition, there were the first-aid classes under the umbrella of the St John Ambulance Brigade and the Guinness Athletic Union – two of his most successful ventures.

A number of factors contributed to the growth of the social scene at St James's Gate: the sheer number of people, many with similar interests; the great degree of inter-marriage within Guinness circles; and the encouragement by the company of social contact. Indeed, this was achieved very successfully, despite the barriers between the working classes and management, and people's different social and religious backgrounds. At the level of the social clubs, whether athletic or arts-based, there was always a comfortable interaction between all the members.

In the 1930s and 1940s, one of the first moves into the arts was the formation of the St James's Gate Literary and Debating Society. This developed in a number of ways, ranging from looking at books to sharing opinions and producing plays. Television had yet to arrive in Ireland, and in Dublin at the time attendance at plays was a popular activity and one of the popular forms of leisure activity was the reading of books. There were many public libraries in Dublin, the nearest to the brewery being in Thomas Street, with others within walking distance at Kevin Street and Inchicore. There had also been an extensive library and reading room in the workmen's rooms in Belview since about 1905. In addition, for those who didn't have time to go to the public libraries, there were small libraries situated in the corners of local shops; a small fee of a few pence was charged for the borrowing of a book.

At St James's Gate, a major incentive involved the site at the corner of James's Street and Watling Street – more correctly the original 'St James's Gate' as it stood in Middle Ages – was developed into a five-hundred-seat theatre, as described earlier, complete with balcony, space for a bar or reception area, a large stage with an overhead scenery dock, an orchestra pit at the front of the stage, and a 1950s state-of-the-art lighting scheme and amplification unit by Strand Electric. In the main foyer hung a portrait of Lord Iveagh, and on a huge wall over the stairs there was a Landseer painting entitled 'Stag at Bay'.

An example of the difference between the social classes of the time was the fact that there were bench seats in the stalls area of the theatre and individual seats in the balcony area. This was not a Guinness phenomenon, however, but a layout common to theatres and cinemas throughout Dublin in that era. In these establishments, there was seating of various quality to match the prices being charged. Cinema seats, for example, started at fourpence for wooden seats and rose to 2/6 (two shillings and sixpence) for the 'luxury' seats. It was said at the time that miracle cures could be achieved by going to the fourpenny seats. One Dublin wit of the time said that you could 'go in lame and come out walking' (with fleas!).

For industrial Ireland of the 1950s the Rupert Guinness Hall was a huge leap forward: it was used not only for entertainment purposes but also as a conference centre. The facilities, which included a highly professional catering department, were second to none in Ireland. The hall was used on a regular basis by the Board for conference and training purposes. In addition, it was used by the Medical Department for public-information lectures and it became, later in the 1950s, a centre for the Blood Transfusion Board, which visited the brewery once a year to collect blood donations from the workforce. When this happened, the seats in the stalls were removed to make way for the stretcher beds used for blood donations. Of course, the 'tonic drink' afterwards mostly consisted of bottles of stout supplied by the company.

The Rupert Guinness Hall was used mainly in its first ten years for the Annual Entertainment, which took place in January each year. Other users at the time included the Drama Group, the Choir and the Film Society.

THE GUINNESS DRAMA GROUP

The drama group evolved from the Literary and Debating Society. In 1948, a number of members of this society, some of whom were members of the Shakespearian Society in Dublin, came together to establish a group for the production of plays. Founding members of the Drama Group included Audrey Braca, Yvonne Robins and Jack Bolger.

The first production of the group was Lennox Robinson's *The Whiteheaded Boy*. As the Rupert Guinness Hall had not yet been built, this took place in the theatre of the Royal Irish Academy of Music in Westland Row on 23 and 24 May 1949. The producer was Jack Bolger, the stage manager was Ken Brayden, and the cast included Pat Monaghan, Des Brennan, Jimmy Hayden, Ethel Sargent, Pauline Parker, Audrey Braca,

Ken Brayden, June Learmont, Oliver D'Arcy, Liam Foynes, Yvonne Robins and Phyllis Maher. Interval music was provided by an orchestra, which was led by Norman Rankin and included Bernadette Cervana, Ena Monks, Gertie O'Brien and Colette Redmond. Other locations used for the production of plays included the theatre in the grounds of Our Lady's Hospice in Harold's Cross.

In 1951, for the inaugural show to open the Rupert Guinness Hall, the Drama Group came together with a newly formed Musical Society and members of the Annual Entertainment variety group to present the 'First Entertainment at the Rupert Guinness Hall' from 16 to 19 May 1951. The Drama Group presented *The Shadow of a Gunman* by Sean O'Casey. The producer was Jack Bolger, the stage manager was Tom Rossiter and lighting was by Harry Ledwidge. The Variety Group presented entertainment by Eddie Bannon and Jimmy McDonagh and a short sketch written by Harry Carrick, entitled *Rejuvenation*. The Musical Society finished off the evening with a flourish by presenting *Trial by Jury* by Gilbert and Sullivan. The producer and conductor was Victor Leeson. The programme credits all costumes to Violet Cummins, made by Gings Theatrical Stores in Dame Street, Dublin.

During the 1950s and 1960s, the Drama Group quickly established itself as one of the foremost in the Irish amateur drama scene. There was an important name change in the early 1960s when the group became 'The Guinness Players'. Plays were produced at least twice a year, and once a year a play was entered for the various drama festivals in the country. The Players quickly established a reputation as one of the best groups in the country, and there was a demand from organisers of drama festivals around the country for them to take part. As a result, the Guinness Players won many first-place awards, as well as best actor/best actress awards. The names of the successful casts appeared in the news pages of the provincial and national newspapers; they included Marie Geoghegan, Jimmy McClatchie, Yvonne Robins, Dominic Greer and Michael

Kiersey. The casts always included a mix of management and workers working together with the intention of giving the performances of their lives.

In 1959, the Players came to prominence with the world amateur première of John Osborne's *Look Back in Anger,* produced by Louis Lentin, and in 1961 Ray MacAnally produced *The Waters of the Moon.* The Guinness Players, under the creative directorship of Paddy Ryan, entered the amateur drama circuit in 1962 with *The Queen and the Rebels* by Ugo Betti. The group went on to win the All-Ireland Drama Award a number of times. In 1967, they won with Paddy Ryan's production of *All My Sons* by Arthur Miller. Also, in 1968 they produced two plays, *The House of Bernarda Alba,* with Heather Hewson in the lead role, and *Waiting for Godot,* starring Dominic Greer and Jimmy McClatchie.

As an amateur drama group, the Players had a number of advantages. Firstly, amongst the population of the Brewery, there was a vast range of talents which could be drawn upon. Indeed, the graduates who joined the No. 1 staff from UCD or Trinity College included Norman Rodway and Des Keogh, who, in their amateur days, were members of the Guinness Drama Group. An equally important advantage for the group was the availability of the Rupert Guinness Hall for rehearsals. While other drama groups in the country had to rent draughty rooms for rehearsals, the Guinness group could walk from their work across James's Street, into the hall and onto the stage on which the play was going to be presented. The scenery and props could also be designed and constructed in situ with the occasional help of Guinness engineers who were close at hand. Finally, when the play was taken on tour to the amateur drama festivals, a Guinness truck could be hired by the group for a nominal fee. From the company's point of view, a truck driving around the country in Guinness livery promoted the company in many towns and villages in Ireland.

The Guinness family always maintained an interest in the progress of the Drama Group; for some time, the patron of the group was Bryan Guinness, Lord Moyne, who attended all first nights and also attended committee meetings. Lord Moyne would, at least once a year, throw a magnificent party in his Dublin house at Knockmaroon for his social set and, in his capacity as patron of the Drama Group, would invite ten or twelve members of the group. On many of these occasions, he would plan the evening so that the Drama Group would be asked to plan and prepare a short excerpt from a classical play for his guests. Over the years, this became a regular feature of the group, so that Lord and Lady Moyne came to know many of the group on a personal level. My personal experience is one of being asked to attend with a group to take part in an excerpt of a play he had written himself. Not only did he and his wife welcome us, but his children were there to take guests' coats, offer drinks and see that everyone was well received. In addition, on learning that I had recently been married, he asked to meet my wife, who was with the group, and he wished us well.

From the late 1960s, several changes were made to the group. The key players had become so good at their parts that it became difficult for an inexperienced person to join the group. As a result of a motion at an AGM, a 'young' Guinness Players was formed, to become a nurturing base for future talent. The establishment of this group led to an influx of members from across the social spectrum of the company, all of whom were completely inexperienced when it came to acting. This resulted in a first production by the group and produced a cohesive group which, for the next decade, formed the backbone of a revitalised Guinness Players.

By the 1980s, not only had television come to stay, but there had also been a huge increase in the programming budgets available to the Irish TV stations. For many members of the public, going to the theatre to see a play became a less attractive proposition.

THE GUINNESS VARIETY GROUP

All over Ireland, the amateur drama festivals had a new rival: a 'Tops of the Town' variety show (sponsored by a major tobacco company) was being produced by many employers around the country to encourage their employees to participate socially. These shows required huge financial backing, which they got from the companies. Also, they attracted many more participants: there were opportunities for singers, dancers, musicians and comedians, as well as the background people who wrote the scripts, painted the scenery and made the lavish costumes.

As 'Tops of the Town' came into being in the 1980s, a new group was formed in Guinness, and the Guinness Players found themselves sharing dates in the Rupert Guinness Hall not only for the shows but also for rehearsal evenings. Later, there was a shift of people from drama to variety. Part of the reason for this was that a variety show had parts for more people and gave better opportunities for newcomers to display their talents. By the mid-1990s, the Guinness Players had few members, and there was a last production of *Dangerous Corner* by J. B. Priestley, produced by Yvonne Robins. By then, the 'Tops of the Town' competition had lost momentum and the Guinness Variety Group had renamed itself 'Arthur's Team'. In this format, the Variety Group continued to produce many shows with energy, commitment and talent into the twenty-first century.

THE GUINNESS CHOIR

This had its origins, as did the Guinness Players, in the 1950s St James's Gate Drama Group. The choir's founder, Victor Leeson, was a prominent member of the Drama Group. In December 1951, Victor produced Handel's oratorio *Samson,* which was the first major presentation of the newly structured 'St James's Gate Musical Society'. This was also the first production of many in which the Society employed soloists – in this case at the rate of five guineas a night. As was to be expected from the high standard set by Victor, not just for the performers but also for himself, this production received an excellent review in the *Irish Press*. In the first five years, the choir sang mainly operettas, but it changed style in 1956 with a performance of Haydn's *The Seasons*. In 1958, the choir gave what is thought to be the first concert performance in Ireland of Bach's *St Matthew Passion*.

Until his retirement in 1984, the choir enjoyed hugely creative and energetic leadership from Victor Leeson. In the programme notes of Haydn's *Die Schopfung* for the fortieth-anniversary concert, Tony Perrem describes Victor's characteristic style:

> His sense of style and taste were unimpeachable. With his great talent, and above all his intergrity and spirituality, one instinctively knew that you were in the presence of authencity, in the real sense of that word. . . . I held him in nearly equal measures of trust, respect, frustration, awe, gratitude, love and affection.

In the early 1960s, Victor Leeson offered classes in music appreciation, held after working hours, for anyone who wished to attend. To a small group of eager students, he played classical LPs on a portable record player, which he himself had brought into the dressing-room area of the Rupert Guinness Hall. As he played each piece, he stopped the music at intervals to describe how the composer had worked and reworked the piece. He gave remarkable insights into classical music to an attentive audience.

Following Victor's retirement in 1984, the choir continued to tackle choral works under the direction of John Dexter and several guest conductors, including Albert Rosen, Proinnsias O'Duinn and Bryden Thompson. David Milne became musical director in 1991; under his direction, the choir celebrated its fiftieth anniversary in 2001 with a gala concert in the National Concert Hall.

The Guinness Film Society

This society, which was a branch of the Irish Film Society, came into being sometime in the 1950s – a period of rigid censorship in the film industry in Ireland. Founder members included Olive Kingston and Audrey Braca. The Irish Film Society was founded in the early 1950s and was able, as a private society with its own members, to source films directly from the distributors and to show them to its members without a censor's certificate. Thus, the Society was able to import and show films from all over the world that would have had little chance of being shown publicly for either commercial or censorship reasons.

Each year, the honorary secretary of the Guinness Film Society would meet with other branch representatives of the Irish Film Society and choose a programme of films for the forthcoming winter season. The cost of importing each film could then be shared with the branches and the film duly passed from Guinness to UCD, from UCD to Cork, from there to Galway, and so on.

Meanwhile, back at Guinness, the announcement of the programme of films was an eagerly awaited piece of news. Once the programme had been announced, the membership tickets sold like hot cakes. To be a committee member meant that you were a popular person; it was the plan of the committee to ensure that each area of the Brewery site was represented on the committee. After the tickets had sold out, the Rupert Guinness Hall was booked for the relevant dates and the electricians' shop contacted to ensure that a projectionist would be available, since the projector in the hall was a piece of the company's electrical equipment. On one occasion, the electrician rostered for the job of showing the film objected to the film on moral grounds and had to be replaced!

The night of each showing was a big social occasion, as most members had subscribed for a double ticket and brought along their girlfriends, boyfriends or spouses. Committee members would check tickets and distribute a handout on the film. During the interval, members would be given details of the collection for the orphans' Christmas party. When the show was over, most of the roughly four hundred cinemagoers would retire to the various pubs in Thomas Street to continue the chat and to discuss the film.

In the 1960s, the Film Society branched out into the realm of filmmaking. A junior film-production team was invited to the 1963 Berlin Film Festival to make a film about the divided city. Those on that team included Johnny Gleeson, Cecil Coyne, Noel Earley, Max Mulvihill, Liam Keane, Margaret Egan, Anne Hughes and the current writer. That visit turned out to a memorable one, as the week the group were there President John F. Kennedy arrived in Berlin and made his famous 'Ich bin ein Berliner' speech.

Later films produced by the group included the award-winning *Liffey Faces,* produced by Mike Lawlor and filmed by Reis Heik, and *Ciall Ceannaigh,* a light-hearted look at shopping in Cornelscourt.

OTHER SOCIAL ACTIVITIES

Each year there was a flurry of activity surrounding the Christmas parties hosted by various departments. Invariably, the focus was on the whether certain eligible and attractive young ladies would attend: those blessed with such attention were invited to every party, whether on or off the premises. At another level, there were informal parties hosted by foremen, supervisors and managers. Eventually, the board of directors, for various good reasons – there was a serious car accident following one party – forbade the holding of such parties. The director who issued the directive not to hold such parties, John Davies, became known in Guinness folklore as 'The man who cancelled Christmas'.

Partying continued, however, in the various pubs in Thomas

Street, the most notable being Hannans, Ryans and Lynches. In these premises, there would always be several parties going on in different parts of the pub: it was just possible to take part in two or three parties at the same time by moving between them. In the case of Lynches, the unique layout of the premises meant that people who wanted to move between the bar and the lounge had to go out into the street and re-enter through another door or – as happened mostly – take a short cut through the gents' toilet.

11

Working on Shift

The main lesson to be learned from working on shift, whether in Guinness or not, is the value of teamwork – or the lack of it. All human life is there. People who work from nine to five generally see their colleagues within a set timeframe, where most are on their best behaviour. Most wear clothes that are semi-formal and present themselves with reasonable standards of appearance and personal hygiene. This was not necessarily so on shift in Guinness during the labour-intensive days which preceded the mechanisation of the 1990s.

In the Guinness Brewery, most shift work was divided into three shifts every twenty-four hours, seven days a week, fifty-two weeks a year. There were therefore three shifts, but the personalities that made up the team were not constant. As a result, you got to work with diverse groups of people, some good, others not so good. Yet, for every team, there were similar targets to be met. Inevitably, there were personality clashes on some teams, while others ran extremely well.

Team members' personalities covered the whole spectrum, from the intense to the jokers, and those who were never to be found when you wanted them. Disagreements on shift could be most intense but, by the end of the shift, targets had to be met, and the objective was to 'get the job done'. Disputes which seemed insoluble at the time could be referred up the line to the manager and the union representative, to be resolved later.

Appearances could be, at best, unique. Protective gloves

could be used creatively to conceal a glass of pilfered beer. Locks on sample cocks – taps on the sides of vats and associated pipework from which laboratory samples were drawn – could become 'broken' yet appear to be locked. A notebook introduced by management for the purpose of writing up which valves had broken locks had numerous comments written into it, culminating with the statement that 'all the men are locked'.

The company also had a number of secure stores which were used to hold bottles of Guinness of various ages and strengths. These were for sampling purposes, by both the laboratory and the tasting panel. Needless to say, some bottles 'found their way' into the pockets of the workers. One story told is of the man walking through the gate on his way home, with a bottle in his pocket. The bottle fell out of his pocket and smashed on the ground. 'Who threw that?' was his quick retort.

Jokers abounded on shift. Jokes ranged from sending a younger colleague for the proverbial 'bucket of steam' to 'the long weight' (wait) or 'the long stand'. Many boys remember being sent to the 'jacks clerks' (the lavatory attendants) to request 'the daily returns, both in volume and weight'. Many close friendships developed on shift. Common ground was found in discussions at breaks or mealtimes. Sport was a usual topic, with enthusiasts being 'slagged' over their favourite team or sport. Interests were shared on topics such as politics, history, music and the arts.

Nonetheless, working together on shift generated a hothouse atmosphere in which the balance found in the world outside was sometimes lost. If a particular problem was identified on, say, the night shift, and reported by note to the relevant people on the day shift, and the problem was not fixed by the next night, all hell broke loose. Being apart from the mainstream generated a form of paranoia which was evident in people becoming extremely annoyed over small things.

Similarly, annoyance with personalities reached proportions not generally understood by those unused to shift work. People with strange personality traits were lampooned and jeered behind their backs with all the enthusiasm of children at boarding school. When the victim was a manager or shift manager, the tales about him were whispered behind his back and, sometimes, to his face.

It must be emphasised that the most stabilising influence when it came to shift work were the foremen and those on the next grade below them, the chargehands, known as 'chargers'. These were incredibly loyal, hard-working and meticulous in their duties at all times. Their job was to ensure that the essential checks were in place before the shift manager appeared in the plant – described as being 'on the floor'. As a shift manager, once you were told that the plant was ready to begin, you could be assured that this was so. Then, once the process had begun, you could attend to other duties, in the knowledge that the plant was in safe hands.

One particular feature amongst shift managers before the 1990s was the use of the Guinness house, 101 James's Street, as a form of residence for shift staff. Its use for this purpose began in the early 1900s to enable staff to be on call for the production areas. This was related to a chainlike system of decision-making which required most decisions to be made by either the manager or the duty manager and then handed down through the system.

The house at 101 James's Street was a redbrick three-storeyed building over a basement with three entrances – the front door, the basement door and the back door. The basement housed the housekeeper and her staff and contained a kitchen, a laundry room and some storage rooms. On the ground floor were two living rooms, one for the senior (generally Brewhouse) staff, the other for the juniors. This floor also contained a small number of bedrooms. The first and second floors housed several bedrooms, two bathrooms and two toilets. Each bedroom contained a single old-fashioned bed, a crockery basin and a jug of cold water for washing, and a towel. The baths in the bathrooms were free-standing and extraordinarily large.

Shift management could use the living rooms while on shift to relax on breaks, seated in armchairs. It was the place to go for 'a shower and a shave'. In wintertime, there was a fire in the grate. Stories abound about whose duty it was to stoke the fire: folklore tells us that the senior man on duty would phone the junior man in the plant to come over, stoke the fire and put more coal on it. There are also stories of junior staff who were not allowed in the living room breaking in, taking over the plush armchairs and stealing the *Financial Times!*

The bedrooms were in use until the early afternoon. Staff whose roster began at 5 or 6 AM could sleep in a bedroom overnight and be called by security in time to begin their shift. Then, staff whose night duty finished at 6 AM could use another bedroom to sleep for six or eight hours, be called by the housekeeper at an agreed time and be given breakfast on a tray before returning home. The housekeeper then had an opportunity to clean and restock the rooms in the afternoon.

The keys to the front door of '101' were treasured items. Firstly, they were a status symbol, indicating that the holder was a trusted member of staff. Secondly, a key could give full access to the house when the person was off-duty: some people seemed to live there, and plenty of mischief happened during the hours of darkness.

The kitchen of '101' was also a popular place, particularly late at night. The grill was always on, cooking bacon, sausages and toast, and there were endless cups of tea and coffee for those arriving in from town, from the pubs, as well as those who just wanted supper before retiring for the night. One often wonders how the housekeeper kept the place in order and a stock of food in the fridge.

On the subject of food, one of the advantages of shift work was the wonderful food served in the staff dining room. For those on the early shift there was breakfast at 8 AM, for those on the late shift there was dinner at 7 PM, and for those on the night shift there was a dinner at 11 PM. At one stage, there were also kitchens in mess rooms around the plant to which food was sent to be cooked as required by those on shift. Eventually, for reasons of health and hygiene, these kitchens were closed and everyone on shift was required to eat in the dining room.

The Belview Dining Rooms

For many generations of Guinness workers, meals were provided from early morning until teatime in the Workmen's Dining Rooms in Belview. Since the days of Sir John Lumsden and the concerts, the 'rooms' had always been a centre of social activity. While breakfasts and teas were provided at the appropriate times, the main emphasis was on a well-balanced 'dinner' in the middle of the day for thousands of men. From noon onwards, these men streamed into the dining room and were seated at long tables, where they had a four-course meal for a shilling, and there was always a 'special' for one shilling and ten pence.

Perhaps the best tribute to the dining room was the graffiti seen on the wall of the cylinder filling plant in the 1980s, when the currency had changed to decimal and the shilling had become fivepence. There were ongoing discussions on a retirement plan, and it was apparent that large numbers would be offered retirement:

> *From the brewery they say we are going,*
> *We'll miss the free beer and OT,*
> *But especially the rooms up in Belview,*
> *Where the dinners are only 5p!*

The Taps

Drinking on shift was a continuous problem for many. In less enlightened days, the company gave an allowance of two pints of beer per day, to be consumed on the premises. Thus, instead of a tea break, as with other jobs, operators took a 'beer break'. For these breaks, workers went to an internal bar called 'the Tap'.

There were several 'taps' around the site. Problems occurred when the imbibers spent too much time at the tap and, on their return, did not take too kindly to being reprimanded. One reason for spending too much time at 'the Tap' was when workers met staff from other departments and discussions developed into good craic.

There is a story told about the night shift in the Brewhouse one night in the 1970s. Lord Boyd of Merton, who was married to the Hon. Patricia Guinness, had been appointed to the Board, and the family had been given temporary accommodation in 98 James's Street, across from the Front Gate. Late at night, Lord Boyd, being an affable person, decided that he would pay a surprise visit to the night shift. He arrived in the Brewhouse sometime after midnight and was received in a friendly manner by those on shift.

The workers offered to take him to the Tap for a pint – on condition that, being a director, he would sign a docket for additional beer. In due course, he signed the docket, but he neglected to state on the docket the number of pints or the date. Needless to say, a good time was had by all! Then the docket was pinned up on the wall and for several days afterwards every worker who came into the Tap was able to draw an additional pint (or more!) based on what went into Brewery folklore as 'the Long Docket'!

In addition to drinking the beer allowance of two pints, many succumbed to the temptation of pilfering beer from various parts of the process. Detection of such pilfering – a sackable offence – was a constant problem for foremen and shift managers. The situation occasionally got out of hand and it required much wisdom to reach an equitable compromise. Many men had the appetite to consume a large amount on shift. Where it came from was next to impossible to prove!

In due course, several courses of action solved the problem. Firstly, the company replaced the beer allowance with a docket arrangement for a case of beer in bottle or can every two weeks, to be consumed off the premises. Secondly, many of the heavier drinkers developed health problems and were replaced on shift by younger men who had more of an interest in their health than in drinking beer. Thirdly, the brewing process came to be done in stainless-steel vessels which were completely enclosed, thus eliminating all opportunity for sampling the product illicitly.

FUNNELS AND TUNNELS

In the early twentieth century, the site at St James's Gate was a fascinating and magical place. The site, which was on three levels, covered sixty-two acres and consisted of numerous buildings on various public streets. The 'upper level' consisted of the area around Robert Street, the Storehouse and the Brewhouse. The 'middle level' covered the front offices, and the 'lower level' was the area north of James's Street, purchased by the company in 1873. These areas were connected in many ways. There was the popular and scenic narrow-gauge steam railway, which ran from the southerly extremity of the site at the Grand Canal harbour at Robert Street right through the various buildings, then descended through a spiral tunnel from the upper to the lower level.

The buildings were also connected at a high level by pedestrian bridges. It was therefore possible to walk from one building to the next, following the process flow, without going out into the street – thus avoiding the need for security checks. One particular bridge connected the Brewhouse to the Storehouse. This was a wide bridge with a wall down the centre, so that the tour guides could walk groups of visitors across one side and avoid the other side, which contained an open-air lavatory with some covered cubicles.

More mysterious were the underground tunnels which crisscrossed the whole site. Like the bridges, these connected most of the buildings and were used principally to carry beer pipes (or 'mains'). These existed mainly at the upper level: up to the late

1800s, the lower level was not part of the Guinness site. The tunnels were dark, dingy and damp. They were slippery underfoot and could, at times, be flooded. The lighting was unreliable and it was always wise to carry a torch when traversing them.

In addition to these small tunnels there were three main tunnels, constructed in the late 1800s, which crossed under James's Street, connecting the upper and lower levels. The oldest was the spiral tunnel for the narrow-gauge railway system, which spiralled two and a half times before emerging into the bright lights of the lower level. Close to that was a pedestrian tunnel to which access was gained by descending several flights of stairs.

By far the most important and most modern of these tunnels was the one which connected the main brewery yard with the power station. This was a high circular structure which carried steam and hot water from the power station to the main brewing areas. It also carried beer pipes from the Vathouse to the Tank Station, the Kegging Plant and the Racking Shed. This tunnel had to be inspected by the shift managers every time beer was pumped from one location to another, to ensure that there were no leaks. It was discovered in the 1970s that not only beer but also the deadly gas carbon dioxide could leak from these pipes. Following the tragic deaths in 1972 of engineer Bill Rufli and plumber Gerry Donnelly from suffocation, measures were put in place to ensure that CO_2-detection precautions were always in place.

THE EXCISE OFFICERS

An integral part of the brewing process was the presence of the Excise Officers. These were civil servants, representing the government, whose job was to endure that the company paid excise duty on the alcohol content of the Guinness. Up to the 1990s, this duty was levied at the start of fermentation on the basis that the (then) unfermented liquid contained the potential for a calculated volume of alcohol. The declared volume and strength of the final product was calculated by the brewing staff based on what was called a 'dry dip' of the vessel. This was the depth in inches from the 'door' (top opening) of the vessel to the surface of the liquid.

But, with the huge size of the vessels (one vessel had the capacity to hold nineteen double-decker buses!), this measurement could be quite imprecise. A deviation of even one inch could mean a huge gain for the government and a subsequent loss for the company – or the other way round.

In such matters, the social skills of the excise officer and the shift manager became important, to ensure that all declarations were fair and accurate. Any disputes, for whatever reason, could have serious consequences, as the declaration and the process would be delayed. Moreover, the fermentation process could not be stopped and later dips taken would be further unreliable due to the generation of gas.

Later in the brewing process, it became extremely important to ensure that every gallon of beer was accounted for. Excise duty had already been paid, and the brew was a valuable commodity. If there were any beer losses (such as an accidental loss down the drain), the first person to be called was the excise officer, so that the loss could be verified and measured and a claim prepared for the repayment of the duty on the brew.

Inevitably, from time to time there were serious losses of beer down the drain due to human error. This was the worst happening that could be imagined for someone on duty in the Brewing Department. As a precautionary procedure, whenever beer was being transferred along pipework to another vat or another department, all valves and pipes along the route would be checked and sometimes double-checked. This led to overzealousness on the part of some people, including the individual who was seen talking to the valves above his head, saying: 'You're closed, you're open.' Another gentleman failed to close a drain valve in a particularly dark corner of the Vathouse, and after a large quantity of beer was lost on his shift, the said drain was named 'Jeremy's Hole'. In another's case, his boastful catch-phrase was: 'It didn't happen on my shift.'

THE APPLIANCE OF SCIENCE

For the first fifty years of the twentieth century, the technology of brewing changed very little. Many of the processes were manual, and the brewing industry was labour-intensive. As Ireland moved out of the recession of the 1950s, a series of changes took place in brewing technology which reduced the amount of hard physical labour required of brewery workers in general and thus reduced the numbers required to staff the brewery at St James's Gate. Technical changes were also introduced for reasons of quality, both in terms of quality control and quality assurance. (Quality control refers to quality checks on beer that has already been brewed, whereas quality assurance refers to systems and procedures which are put in place to 'assure' that all quality-control results fall within pre-set limits.)

Many of the technological changes were initiated in the Research and Development Department. (This department had a workshop behind locked doors to which access could only be gained by ringing a bell and explaining the purpose of your visit. In many ways, it resembled M's workshop in the James Bond films.) One example of such change was the introduction of a trial widget, pioneered in the early 1960s, put into cans of Guinness to create the perfect head. As with the current system, this was based on a tiny capsule inside the can which released the gas when the can was opened. Cans of Guinness with widgets were not launched onto the market for several decades, however, due to the need to carry out further research into the gas mix required and, in particular, into polymer science.

Other technological changes included the standardisation of draught Guinness. Before this approach was adopted, bar staff in pubs had to pull a pint using a combination of casks and taps of beers of different ages. This new process involved the introduction of a standard amount of nitrogen and carbon dioxide to give a consistent head on the pint. One man in particular stands out as a technological genius of the time: Sammy Hildebrand, who had a most incisive and enquiring mind, spearheaded many of the company's major technical projects, such as developing methods for sterilising vessels and pipes effectively.

To the customer, the most visible change in Guinness – seen in the late 1950s – was the change from wood to metal casks. Wooden casks were difficult to clean and almost impossible to sterilise, because wood is porous and bacteria could reside in small internal cracks which could not be reached using steam. Metal casks required less maintenance, had a longer life, had a tighter capacity range, and could be steam-sterilised. Nonetheless, they required a large workforce to move them and fill them. After some years, they were replaced by metal kegs, because the movement of metal casks was labour-intensive and liable to cause work-related injuries.

As metal kegs were uniform in size and straight-sided, they could be moved by mechanical means. They could also be bulk-handled by forklift trucks. The original kegs were made of aluminium and, after some years, were found to be prone to corrosion. Hence the final move to stainless-steel kegs.

The transportation of bulk quantities of beer to bottlers also went through several phases, many designed to use labour more efficiently. The first use of bulk tankers was of road tankers. Later, the company moved to cylindrical 504-gallon transportable trucks which could be lifted on and off flat-bed trailers by forklift truck. Eventually, there was a return to road tankers.

Around the same time, in order to facilities deliveries from Guinness in Dublin to England, the company had two tanker ships built. The first of these was a conversion of *The Lady Patricia,* which had previously carried 504-gallon tanks and was modified to carry on-board vats. These vats were filled with beer from road tankers, each of which had a capacity of 4,680 gallons, at City Quay, facing the Custom House and close to Dublin's Financial Services Centre.

The Guinness berth at City Quay had seen many changes over a sixty-year period. This began in 1875 when casks were transported on flat-bed wagons through the Brewery gates on Victoria Quay, near Heuston Station, to a Guinness jetty on the river edge. They were then loaded into barges and transported down-river to City Quay and Custom House Quay, from where they were lifted into the holds of the Guinness ships. The last Guinness barge sailed down the Liffey on 21 June 1961.

The Lady Patricia sailed to Runcorn on the Manchester Ship Canal with a full capacity of fifty tanker-loads – equivalent to 234,000 gallons of beer – and the beer was pumped into English road tankers on the quayside there. The technology used in the process was so unusual that an edition of the BBC TV programme *Tomorrow's World* was filmed on board *The Lady Patricia* in 1974. In 1977, a purpose-built ship, *Miranda Guinness,* which had an even larger capacity than *The Lady Patricia,* was launched.

This entire process was unique in Guinness history because it involved training the Guinness shipping crews in beer-handling techniques. In parallel, it also meant that a shift manager from St James's Gate was appointed as liaison officer to the ship. His job was to ensure that training was adequate and was constantly updated, and that quality was assured to the standards of St James's Gate and later to ISO 9002. The various shipping crews expanded their skills levels, and some later moved into mainstream operations in the brewery.

Another major Guinness project of the 1970s was Guinness Light. This was a new beer, produced in response to market trends. It was 'light' because it had less hops and a slightly reduced alcohol content. Drinkers had indicated that they would like a beer that had the quality of Guinness but was sweeter and less strong. For many reasons, this beer was unsuccessful in the marketplace. One was that the market was not yet ready for a light beer. Those who had requested it did not buy it, and those who preferred the traditional Guinness scorned it. One Dublin wit is reported to have ordered a pint of Guinness and a pint of Guinness Light by asking for 'A pint of the real stuff, and a pint of the lettin'-on stuff!'

Nonetheless, Guinness Light was a success in the brewing departments. New skills were learnt and perfected by those who were on the project team. New plant and equipment, installed initially for Guinness Light, became essential components of future projects.

Perhaps one of the greatest advances in technology at St James's Gate had its origins in the sterilising process. From the 1950s, great emphasis was placed on the sterilisation of all beer vessels in order to ensure product consistency and quality. This required the sterilisation of all vessels with pressurised steam – a process that generated temperatures in excess of 100°C. This form of sterilisation required an understanding of microbiology as well as a clear grasp of the process of venting vessels to prevent implosion, and called for a dedicated team of operators, based in the Storehouse, called steamers. (One of these was Paddy Skelton, referred to earlier.) These men were unique characters who know every beer vessel and pipe in the entire process. They were on call twenty-four hours a day to sterilise plant anywhere in the Brewery. Thus they had to fit in their work with the main process and, most importantly, with the other operators. This required facilitation and negotiation skills, with which each of them was blessed in large volumes. Their work also required great physical strength, as they had to open and close huge steam valves in conditions of great heat and humidity.

Eventually, the work of the steamers was replaced. With increased confidence in the use of chemical cleaners and sterilants, processes were adapted for their use, thus reducing the need for high-pressure steam. The use of cleaners and sterilants, however, necessitated the redesign of vessels to include in-built sprayballs and conical bottoms. (Sprayballs were part of an in-place cleaning system enabling water and sterilants to be sprayed under pressure to cleanse the inside of a beer vessel; conical bottoms were designed to collect the yeast which deposited at the bottom of the vessels at the conclusion of the fermentation process.) These innovations were to form the basis for the design of brewing vessels in the future.

CONCLUSION

LOOKING TO THE FUTURE

The Guinness Brewery at St James's Gate has always had an eye to the future. Otherwise, it would not have succeeded for two and a half centuries. On the other hand, dealing with future events requires particular management skills, which, from time to time, were not easy to find at Guinness.

As a family business in the late eighteenth century and throughout the nineteenth century, the business of the Brewery was continually expanding, thanks to the management skills of the Guinness family. As we have seen, as an ethical Christian family, they saw their wealth from the business as a gift from God, and one which was to be shared with not only their workers but also the city of Dublin, and also with Ireland and England in general. As astute employers, they invested their family fortunes in people as well as in their own illustrious homes and estates.

Into the twentieth century, Guinness steered a wise course through the political unrest in Ireland, the two World Wars, and the emerging economic miracles in Ireland, which resulted from the initiatives of Sean Lemass and others in the late 1950s. As the British Empire declined, Guinness was one of the first large companies to build breweries in new independent countries, investing in the economies of Nigeria, Malaysia and Ghana, among others.

But as the company entered the 1970s, new forms of management were needed. In the operation of the Dublin brewery in particular, new forms of processing and cost control were urgently needed. In conjunction with new technology, new forms of personnel management and accounting were developed. Costs came under the spotlight and were viewed in relation to the future of the company. Comparisons were made with other less-costly breweries, and the view was taken that personnel costs needed to be reduced. Thus began the road to huge change.

In 1973, there was a major reduction in personnel at St James's Gate, which saw several thousand workers given compulsory early retirement. This resulted in a huge loss of skills and expertise at the company. In other circumstances, the workers might have welcomed this move, but in a period in which the company was doing well, they were completely unprepared for it. Retirement without adequate preparation was difficult for many, and those who remained in the Brewery had to endure changes in work practices. Attitudes among the workers hardened, and the company experienced its first strike in its history in 1974.

Following the strike, a number of measures were put in place to create a spirit of involvement amongst the workers. A workers' council – the Brewery Council – was put in place, with committees set up to consider topics ranging from communication to welfare and safety. Thus began many years of committee meetings, which produced various degrees of success. The chairmanship of the council was rotated by agreement with the various trade unions; the first job of the council was to persuade one union group, which had stayed outside the structure, to join up.

Through the 1980s, there were two other retirement plans, reducing personnel numbers further. Under these plans, voluntary retirement was offered to eligible workers. Other changes at the Brewery in the 1980s included the granting of company shares to workers as an annual bonus. Additional shares could also be purchased, within certain constraints. In the case of the profit-share allocations, shares had to be held for a minimum specified period before they could be sold.

At company-director level, there were many changes in the 1980s. Benjamin Guinness retired as Managing Director but remained as a Board member. A marketing director from Nestlé, Ernest Saunders, took over as Managing Director. Several people from the London 'city scene' were appointed to the Board. After a financial crisis related to insider trading, and a high-profile court case, Saunders and several of his fellow directors were deposed, and some, including Saunders, were jailed. The chairmanship of the parent company passed to an accepted 'safe pair of hands', Sir Norman McFarlane, and the company's situation gradually returned to an even keel. In the early 1990s, Sir Norman retired, and the post of Chairman was taken over by a career Guinness person, Brian Baldock, who had been with the company all his life. The managing directorship of Guinness Dublin was taken over by Finbarr Flood in 1989.

Within the company, many non-core activities were identified and contracted out. On the processing side, there had been huge investment in plant and process. A new Brewhouse in the mid-1980s led to the creation of a new Fermentation Department in the early 1990s.

The old Vathouse, with its damp, steamy atmosphere, was closed. The new vessels were all chemically cleaned and the process was now programme-controlled. A new state-of-the-art kegging process was put in place. The new processes required far fewer people, but the people they did require needed specific skills.

Thus three new initiatives happened in symphony. First, a new approach to training and development was introduced. Skills audits were undertaken, and training needs were assessed. Training to meet the new brewing specifications was opened to all personnel, resulting in a cross-culture of process, engineering and software people working together to meet the new challenges of brewing for the future.

Quality procedures were formalised in all departments and written up in manuals. Each department appointed a writer to prepare the procedure manuals in consultation with the workers in the department concerned. Auditors from the National Food Centre were invited in to check out procedures, which were then formally endorsed. Eventually, in December 1992, the brewing company achieved the international quality standard, ISO 9002.

Then a new development plan – Plan 2000 – based on a balance of training and development, combined with new work practices, was introduced. The unique feature of this plan was that it was not imposed from the parent company in London but was designed by the management team at Guinness Dublin. The objective was to try to ensure the long-term survival of the Dublin brewery as a premier production unit within the Guinness organisation. The plan was firmly based on the vision that Guinness Dublin was to become the 'best brewery in the world.'[111] Those with more than thirty years' service were given the opportunity to retire after the age of fifty with a reasonable lump sums and an immediate pension. Most importantly, those who remained were completely reskilled, with a focus on both the company and the individual needs of the employee. The company continues to audit on an annual basis the balance of skills and company needs.

In 1997, Guinness became part of Diageo, a huge multinational complex of companies. The company at St James's Gate, as part of that network of companies, continues to shine, with a reputation for quality and responding quickly to market needs. Guinness stout is still produced on the original site at St James's Gate – at the rate of about 18 million pints a week. Meanwhile, part of the old Storehouse at St James's Gate continues to be a heritage centre for Guinness, and welcomed its two-millionth visitor in 2005.

When it mattered, Guinness was an employer of high moral ethics, giving primary care to Irish and, specifically, Dublin people in addition to being an unusually generous employer. Members of the Guinness family became figures of importance in Ireland and Britain due to their philanthropy. Today, with their still-impressive fortune, they continue that work in a discreet way. They can be proud that their original inheritance of £100 was used wisely and that the name of Guinness is still spoken of with awe and respect all over the world.

146

ENDNOTES

Most of the references refer to material in the Guinness Archive, Diageo Ireland, preserved in the Guinness Storehouse, now part of the Diageo Group. For further information on these, please go to *www.guinness-storehouse.com*. (These references are referred to in the footnotes as 'GA', followed by the file reference.)

CHAPTER 1

1 Michelle Guinness, *The Guinness Spirit: Brewers and Bankers, Ministers and Missionaries*

2 ibid.

3 ibid.

4 Patrick Lynch and John Vaisey, *Guinness's Brewery in the Irish Economy, 1759–1876*

5 ibid.

6 ibid.

7 Bryan Guinness, *Guinness 1759–1959,*
GA ref. GDB/CO04/0013.02

8 F. H. A. Aalen, *The Iveagh Trust: The First Hundred Years*

9 ibid.

10 Lord Moyne, 'Supplement to *The Times* 1959',
GA ref. GDB/CO04.04/0013.02

11 GA ref. GDB/CO04.03/0011, GDB/C004.09/002.10

12 Michelle Guinness, op. cit.

13 ibid.

14 Derek Wilson, *Dark and Light: The Story of the Guinness Family*

15 Michelle Guinness, op. cit.

CHAPTER 2

16	Lynch and Vaisey, op. cit.
17	ibid.
18	ibid.
19	ibid.
20	Charles Cameron, *Reminiscences*
21	GA ref. GDB/PE03.01/0582
22	ibid.
23	GA ref. GDB/PE03.01/0582
24	GA ref. GDB/CO06/0100
25	GA ref. GDB/CO06/0101
26	GA ref. GDB/PE03.01/0582(01)
27	GA ref. GDB/CO06/0103
28	ibid.

CHAPTER 3

29	National Archives: Household Schedule of Returns, South Earl Street, 1901
30	Jacinta Prunty, *Margaret Aylward: 1810–1889*
31	Seebohm Rowntree, *Poverty: A Study of Town Life*
32	GA ref. GDB/PE12/0006.02 (1905)
33	Cameron, op. cit., 'Table of earnings and diet in Dublin'
34	ibid.
35	ibid.
36	GA ref. GDB/PE12/0001 (1901)
37	Jacinta Prunty, *Dublin Slums,* p87
38	Dublin Corporation Records, 'Report on Public Health', vol. iii, 1901, pp348, 349
39	ibid., vol. ii, 1895, p700
40	GA ref. GDB/C006/0108
41	Cameron, op. cit.
42	GA ref. GDB/PE12/0001
43	ibid.
44	GA ref. GDB/PE012/001
45	ibid.

46	Prunty, *Dublin Slums 1800–1925,* p.174.
47	GA ref. GDB/PE12/001
48	ibid.
49	ibid.
50	Cameron, op. cit.
51	GA ref. GDB/PE12/001
52	ibid.
53	ibid.
54	ibid.
55	ibid.
56	ibid.
57	GA ref. GDB/PE012/001
58	ibid.
59	ibid.
60	ibid.
61	GA ref. GDB/PE12/0001
62	GA ref. GDB/PE12/0006
63	Cameron, op. cit.
64	GA ref. GDB/PE12/0006.02
65	GA ref. GDB/PE12/0006.02
66	GA ref. GDB/PE12/003
67	GA ref. GDB/PE12/0034
68	GA ref. GDB/CO04.06/005.01

CHAPTER 4

69	GA ref. GDB/PE03/0580
70	*www.newadvent.org*
71	GA ref. GDB/CO04.06/0049.04
72	GA ref. GDB/PE12/0005
73	Ruth Delaney, *The Grand Canal of Ireland*
74	Lynch and Vaisey, op. cit.
75	Cameron, op. cit.
76	GA ref. GDB/PE12/0034
77	GA ref. GDB/C004.03/0011
78	GA ref. GDB/C004.03/0011

79   GA ref. GDB/C004.03/0011

CHAPTER 5

80   GA. ref. GDB/CO04.06/005/0.01
81   ibid.
82   ibid.
83   GA ref. GDB/CO04.06/005/0.10
84   GA ref. GDB/CO04.06/005/0.02
85   ibid.
86   ibid.
87   GA ref. GDB/CO04.06/005/0.04

CHAPTER 6

88   Aalen, op. cit.
89   ibid.
90   GA ref. GDB/PE03.01/0579
91   Aalen, op. cit.

CHAPTER 7

92   GA ref. GDB/PE06/0093
93   GA ref. GDB/PE03.01/0643
94   ibid.
95   GA ref. GDB/PE03.01/0602
96   GA ref. GDB/PE03.01/0457
97   GA ref. GDB/PE03.01/0173

CHAPTER 8

98   Research by W. Mullen, GA ref. GDB/PR10/0017
99   Peter Somerville-Large, *An Irish Childhood*
100   GA ref. GDB/PE03.01/0584
101   GA ref. GDB/CO06.0108

CHAPTER 9

102   GA ref. GDB/PE03.01/0529

103   GA ref. GDB/PE06.03/0093
104   GA ref. GDB/PE06.03/0093
105   ibid.
106   Minute Book 1953–56, Senior Foremen's Association
107   ibid.
108   ibid.

CHAPTER 10

109   GA ref. GDB/CO06/0101
110   *The Harp* magazine, Christmas 1958

CONCLUSION

111   J. Findlater, 'Stimulating a Thirst for Learning: The Case
         of the Guinness Dublin Brewery' (CEDEFOP)

Bibliography

Books

Aalen, F. H. A. *The Iveagh Trust: The First Hundred Years, 1890-1990*. The Iveagh Trust: Dublin, 1990.

Cameron, Charles. *Reminiscences*. Dublin, 1913.

Delaney, Ruth. *The Grand Canal of Ireland*. 1973.

Dennison, S. R. and Oliver McDonagh. *Guinness 1886-1939: From Incorporation to the Second World War*. Cork University Press: Cork, 1998.

Guinness, Edward. *The Guinness Book of Guinness*. Privately published: Bath, England, 1988.

Guinness, Jonathan. *Requiem for a Family Business*. Macmillan: London, 1997.

Guinness, Michelle. *The Guinness Spirit: Brewers and Bankers, Ministers and Missionaries*. Hodder & Stoughton: London, 1999.

Johnston, Mairin. *Around the Banks of Pimlico*. Attic Press: Dublin, 1985.

Kinsella, Thomas. *Blood and Family*. Oxford University Press: Oxford, 1988.

Lynch, Patrick and John Vaisey. *Guinness's Brewery in the Irish Economy 1759–1876*. Cambridge University Press: Cambridge, 1960.

Prunty, Jacinta. *Dublin Slums, 1800–1925: A Study in Urban Geography*. Irish Academic Press: Dublin, 1998.

———. *Lady of Charity, Sister of Faith: Margaret Aylward 1810–1889*. Four Courts Press: Dublin, 1999.

Rowntree, Seebohm. *A Study of Town Life*. York, 1901.

Somerville-Large, Peter. *An Irish Childhood.* Constable: London, 2002.

Wilson, Derek. *Dark and Light: The Story of the Guinness Family.* Orion: London, 1998.

JOURNALS

Dublin Corporation Archives

CEDEFOP (Centre Européen pour la Developpement de la Formation Professionelle) 'Stimulating a Thirst for Learning: The Case of the Guinness Dublin Brewery'. Luxembourg, 2003.

The Harp magazine. Various editions, held in the Guinness Archives.

ARCHIVES

Guinness Archives

National Archives: 1901 and 1911 Census material

INDEX

Annual Entertainment, 60–1, 85, 91, 121, 122
Association of Brewery Employees, 106
Athletic Union, Guinness, 17, 56, 57, 72–7, 97, 119

Bellevue, 35, 38, 57
Belview (see 'Bellevue')
'Beano', the, 26, 80
Beaumont, 23–4, 29, 92
Bicentenary, 90–3
Blue Book, 87–9, 114
Bournville, 55–7
Brewery Council, 118, 144
Burial Society, Guinness, 53

Cadburys, 17, 56, 62, 74
Cameron, Sir Charles, 41–5, 48, 50, 52, 56, 66
Choir, Guinness, 12, 85, 101, 121, 125–6

Dispensary, 35, 45, 62, 63–4, 66–8
Drama Group, Guinness, 91, 101, 121–5

Excise officers, 137–9

Fanciers' Show, 59, 76, 92
Film Society, Guinness, 116, 121, 127–8

Goodbody's tobacco factory, 54, 70

Harp magazine, *The,* 91, 119

ISO 9002, 104, 141, 146
Iveagh Baths, 26, 57, 73
Iveagh Gardens, 81, 89
Iveagh Hostel, 26, 80
Iveagh, Lord, 17, 25, 27, 51, 74–5, 85, 93, 111, 120
Iveagh Trust, 16, 26, 28, 73, 78–80, 81, 89, 112

'jacks clerks', 68, 131

Kenwood, 26–7
Kingsbridge Woollen Mills, 25

La Touche Cup, 76
'lady clerks', 92, 95, 96, 101
Lady Patricia, The (ship), 140, 141
Lady Superintendent, 44, 75, 85, 101–2, 109
Lady Visitor, 35, 64
latrine timekeepers (see 'jacks clerks')
Levers, 17, 62, 74
Lister Institute, 26, 28
Lumsden, Sir John, 12, 16–17, 38–9, 41, 44, 45, 57, 62–3,
        67–8, 70, 72–4, 119, 134

Marrowbone Lane, 18, 43, 63, 70
Medical Department, 16, 18, 36, 38, 61–6, 90, 96, 113, 114, 121
messengers, 66, 97, 98, 99, 107
Miranda Guinness (ship), 141
Musical Society, Guinness, 91, 122, 125
pawn shop, 88
Permanent Building Society, Guinness, 89
Players, Guinness, 12, 85, 122–4, 125
Port Sunlight, 55, 56–7

Queen's Day, 44, 58–60, 76

Rialto Buildings, 38, 73
Richmond Barracks, 70
Rising, the 1916, 68, 70–1, 94, 105
Roll of Honour, 69
Royal Dublin Society, 58, 59, 92
Rowntrees, 17, 62
Rupert Guinness Hall, 27, 60, 76, 84–5, 92, 110, 116, 121–3, 125, 126, 127

St John Ambulance Brigade, 57, 67–9, 70, 119
St Stephen's Green, 24, 25, 30, 86, 113
Senior Foremen's Association, 66, 107–11
South Dublin Union, 15, 70

technical education, 54, 57, 86
Thomas Court houses, 38, 45, 78, 79, 80–1
tuberculosis, 17, 43, 45, 48, 63, 66–7

Variety Group, Guinness, 85, 122, 125

Workers' Union of Ireland, 106–7, 111, 117
World War I, 67
World War II, 18, 19, 82